LETTERS FROM HOME

:

I Loved Ya Before I Even Met Ya

BARRY K. FREE

Revised Edition

1

(LETTERS FROM HOME)

Copyright © 2017 by (BARRY K. FREE)

ISBN:13: 978-1545079492

     10-1545079498

Printed in USA by 48HrBooks (www.48HrBooks.com)

TABLE OF CONTENTS

FOREWORD

On January 24, 2011, Barry's life changed forever. So did the lives of his adult children, Megan and Matthew. Going from just having the symptoms of flu on Friday night, his wife Cheryl died Sunday night, just two days later. Barry watched powerless as the health professionals scrambled to correctly diagnose and then try to treat the rapidly spreading bacterial infection which took her life. Quickly, Barry was faced with making the decision to move his wife from the small rural hospital to a larger, more well equipped one. He urgently called their children to join him and his wife's sister, not knowing that they would very soon be saying their final goodbyes.

Suddenly losing his wife of 35 years and watching his two adult children and spouses figure out how to catch their collective breath at the loss of their mother, and find their footing again in a world without this energetic, loving woman became the beginning of his grief journey. For his own "therapy", Barry began recording his private thoughts. After writing the first section, working in short chapters, he tentatively decided to share with his children and then a few others, and then continued writing covering the first five years.

As he revised some sections, taking out stories that seemed too personal, his writings became the basis of conversations with his children about what each was feeling. His openess gave permission to share and explore questions which may have been too difficult to bring up without his writings. Without setting out to do this intentionally, Barry created a way for his family to keep close and support each other as they moved through the grief process. Now, in publishing the book, Barry very courageously offers a therapeutic guide for others dealing with the sudden loss of a spouse and beloved parent.

In this powerful book, called "LETTERS FROM HOME: I LOVED YA BEFORE I EVEN MET YA" Barry gives us a very touching reflection on his process of coming to terms with the loss of his wife. It is a tribute to the healing process of grief. Barry's straightforward, sometimes self-depreciating style of writing is very personal, down to earth, educational and inspiring. He pulled me in as a reader. I was often moved to tears and then found myself laughing a few paragraghs later. As a professional trained to work with grieving families, his reflections ring very true. He is able to clearly identify and describe what many people feel but may not be able to put into words. Reading Barry's book lets us nod our heads in recognition and allows us a sense of closure to our sorrowful hearts, missing our loved ones and yet knowing we need to accept their loss and find a way to move on.

I appreciate Barry's wisdom, his courage to share his vulnerability and his faith, as well as his sense of humor. He touched my heart and also taught me again about the power of love and speaking our truth to each other.

Dr. Elisabeth Kubler-Ross, in her groundbreaking book, "ON DEATH AND DYING", outlines the five phases of grieving experienced when one learns they are dying: denial, anger, bargaining, depression and acceptance. These stages also apply to the process of grieving the loss of a loved one.

Dr. Granger Westberg expanded this understanding to include 10 stages in what he named "good grief".

1. We are in a state of shock.
2. We express emotion.
3. We feel depressed and very lonely.
4. We may experience physical symptoms of distress.
5. We feel a sense of guilt about the loss.
6. We may become panicky.
7. We are filled with hostility and resentment.
8. We feel a resistance to usual activities.
9. Gradually hope comes through.
10. We struggle to affirm reality.

Barry's journey parallels these established works and gives a personal description for each stage. We know that the grief cycle is unique to each person and that we move through the stages in our own way and on our own timetable. We also know that there is not a right way to grieve. The risk is that we might get caught in a stage of grief and not be able to move forward, putting our lives on hold, sometimes feeling frozen or unable to engage in life fully again. In sharing the first five years of his journey, Barry inspires us to fully grieve our own losses.

I did not have the privilege of meeting Cheryl. I had heard of her through speaking with Barry. I already knew I liked her. Now, after reading his book, I know I would have loved her. This book is a tribute to her life. And a tribute to a healthy, wonderful long term marriage, tragically ended. It is also a book about the courage of a husband and father to face grief head-on for his own recovery and to help their children, as well as others who loved this beautiful, spirited woman, wife, mother, sister and friend. Finally, it is also a book about being brave and vulnerable. I highly recommend it to anyone needing guidance through the stages of sudden death of a spouse or a loved one. It is also a good read for anyone who knows how to love and be loved. Thank you, Barry.

Foreword written by:

Sally Strosahl, M.A., LCPC
Licensed Clinical Professional Counselor
Certified Grief Counselor
Marriage and Family Therapist

FOURTH GRADE

PREFACE

Fourth grade. Everyone was nervous. New teachers. New kids. The only good part of a new school year was getting to see your old buddies at recess. There's John, Larry, Russell, Jackie, Carol, Greg and Tom. Same old bunch. But wait.

Who's the cute blonde in the third row? I've not never seen her before. As we go around the room telling our names, I find out her name is Cheryl. Wow, she's purrty. I think I'm in love and I haven't even met her yet. Guess I'm gonna have to use all my charm on her. I wonder if she likes frogs?

(It was actually the seventh grade before she truly appreciated my "charms". We then "dated" through junior high and high school right up until two years later when we were married. I guess you could say we were the definition of childhood sweethearts)

DECEMBER 21, 1975

INTRODUCTION

This is a story of my life with the only girl I have ever loved, until now. Cheryl Jean Rundle and I were married on December 21st, 1975. She left us on January 24th, 2011. It started as a story about the struggles of learning to do things by yourself and for yourself after so many years of doing things with someone and for someone. And as an attempt to tell my children about what happened to Cheryl and to try and explain how it has changed me and my life. But I found that I couldn't do that without my belief in God finding its way into what I wrote. So it also became a story of faith and my growth in that faith that has kept me going for the last five years. It has taken four years to write, beginning with part one being written from May 1 to June 15th of 2012. Parts two-four were given to my children in three more issues spanning the next three years. Part five was given to them in the form of this book. It seems that I had to live it before I could write it. That's why it took me so long. I had no intention of publishing these letters but as you can see, someone or something has driven me to do just that.

PART ONE

CHAPTER ONE

:

"LETTERS"

To my daughter Megan and her husband Bob, and my son Matthew and his wife Candace,

I have thought about putting some words and thoughts down on paper for the last year. I guess I wasn't ready to do so until now. I've basically been in a state of shock since Mom died. But, now I am ready to tell you some things that I haven't been able to discuss. About Mom. About our life together. About losing her. And about how hard this journey is.

Obviously, I'm not the first person to lose their spouse. I personally know four guys who have lost their wives and several women who have lost their husbands. But I, like a lot of other people I expect, hadn't really thought of how dramatically their lives have changed. Now I know.

Why am I writing this? Right this moment I am not really sure. I am hoping that becomes clear as I continue on. Maybe to explain to my family and friends what my life is like now? I had no idea how much it would change and how unprepared I was for it. Mom used to say that I needed to live "outside my box" more. Well, honey I'm so far outside of it now that I can't even see it!

I also needed to tell the story of Mom's death. I needed to get it straight in my mind before any more of the details escaped me. From my perspective. The way I saw it happen. It just happened so fast that I wasn't keeping up. My life has been turned upside down and is constantly changing. I really need to write these things down. So I am writing you these "letters". As if I were going to actually send them to you. It's old fashioned but that's who I am. As you well know. They are very personal. It is how I feel or felt at the exact moment that I wrote them. Raw and mostly unedited. I may not feel the same way today at all. I sometimes wonder why schools don't offer a class in living life after losing someone very close to you. All of us are going to experience this at some time in our lives. But, losing your spouse is unique compared to other losses. There's no one to go home to at night. And there's no book on getting through it. So I hope telling you of my experiences will prepare you just a little for what may also happen to you one day. You will need faith. And family. And very understanding friends. I don't know how you get through this without those things. I feel very blessed to have them all.

Where do you have a funeral? Who performs the service? Where is your loved one now? Why did this happen to her? To us? These questions and many more are so hard to answer that I just can't imagine not having God and prayer to help get through this process.

Also, I am writing these letters for Mom. I still talk to her often and ask the question, "What would Cheryl do?" I want her to know how much she influenced my life and those around her. She should know how much of a void there is in my life since she passed. "I loved ya before I even met ya". I used to tell her that to

15

make her laugh. Maybe writing this story will help me find a new purpose and a reason to carry on and deal with the toughest job I have ever had. Living without Mom.

Finally, writing a book is on my bucket list. It is right up there with building something that lasts at least five generations and starring on "American Idol". So I have decided to put these letters in the form of a book. I always thought I would write a mystery if I wrote one. Maybe that's what this is. A mystery about how life doesn't always turn out the way you think it will. I hoped Mom and I would grow old together. The real mystery may be whether or not we get to do that in eternity.

CHAPTER TWO

:

THE HISTORY OF OUR TEAM

Mom and I did meet for the first time in the fourth grade at Little York. Her family moved here from Cuba, Illinois when Grandpa Rundle took the job of Ag Instructor at the high school. I think I really did fall in love with Mom that day but it wasn't until junior high that we started going "steady". We dated through high school, then I went off to Western Illinois University and Mom settled in at what is now ShopKo working as a book keeper. I lived in a dorm with a friend of mine from high school the first year. The second year I moved to an apartment with two friends and my brother, Tom, who transferred there from Illinois State. Mom lived in Monmouth and shared an apartment with another friend of ours from high school.

Mom and I decided to get married halfway through my second year at Western, during my Christmas break. As a friend of mine always says, "she was suicidal if she was apart from me too long". (just kidding) As you guys have heard me say, many times, Great Grandma Free never let us forget that we ruined Christmas that year. She had become pretty set in her ways, like we all tend to do, and several functions had to be held at different times than she was used to.

During our last couple of years of dating, Mom and I used to talk about our dreams for the future. They included getting married, having children and hopefully raising them in the farm house on the "home place" that my Grandma and Grandpa lived in. They had told me that they were thinking of moving to town when one of us boys was ready to start farming. On December 21st, 1975 we set about doing what we had dreamed of.

Those early years of our marriage revolved around family, farming and activities at the Belmont Methodist Church. I started farming in the spring of 1976 after finishing an internship with a local electrician. When I came back to the farm that spring, Grandpa Jim began his new career with the local farm service company by becoming the first manager of the new Rozetta fertilizer plant. I think that he wanted to try something different involving agriculture and thought that between Great Grandpa and me we could handle the farming operation. (About ten years later that was actually true). Uncle Tom soon left school too and we farmed together for a couple years before he returned to Western and finished his degree.

Our family had attended Belmont church since it opened in the 1800's. It was still a very active church, but if someone had studied the age of the members, and the trend towards larger farms, they could have predicted the final days. Small, local churches were going away as fast as small farms and small schools.

Mom once said during a sermon she was giving at our church, that I showed her to God at a revival at the local theatre. I can't remember that night specifically. I personally believe that attending our country church and seeing the example that Grandma and Grandpa set, had more influence on Mom than I did. All I know is that Mom and I had become a "team" and we went about trying to live the dreams that we had talked about.

CHAPTER THREE

:

THE BASICS OF MOM

Your Mom was never happier in her life than when she saw you guys, as babies, for the first time. She was made to be a Mom and would have been an even better Grandma. It came naturally to her. She truly needed someone to need her. Growing up in a large family, I think she did not receive a lot of praise for doing a good job at the activities that she was involved in. Children want to know, not just what their limits are but if they are doing something that pleases their parents. I believe that Mom spent her whole life trying to please people without ever realizing that she really was. As time went on, her confidence grew. The absolute dependence on her, when you were helpless babies may have been the first "trigger". And later on, the demands that her job placed on her were keys to her developing her self-esteem. But, it really wasn't until Mom was approved to be on the church session (board) that she really found her place in our church and the community. She had been on several church committees before but hadn't found her place until she became an elder. Apparently, it just wasn't her time to shine yet. It seems that from the moment she gave her first children's sermon, she was energized with ideas about how to reach out to people in the community. Especially the children. From then on there was never a quiet moment in Mom's (or my) life as she strived every day to do God's work. She had found her true home.

As upset as I was about her generosity with money (she was constantly overdrawn), it was equally as hard for me to tell her no. I was pretty sure whose side God was on in that argument. That probably explains how she convinced me, and many others, to help her with her many projects. The Easter Egg Hunt, the Halloween Party, and services at the assisted living facility were just some of her passions. She even managed to get a Community Thanksgiving Day meal started after she was gone! Our church started serving that the fall after she died in 2011 and it continues to this day. We fund a share of it with money from her memorial plus many donations from our church family and community. We have served free turkey, ham and all that goes with it to an average of 140 people on Thanksgiving Day. It is a huge undertaking for our little church, with a lot of the women also hosting their own families on the same day. It would not be possible without a tremendous outpouring of support. Mom would be so happy to see it take place. As I said, the meal is offered free, though many donate money and take their turn on the serving line and washing dishes. We will continue to help with that until the memorial money runs out or when we run out of helpers. The flier that we use for the lunch is on the following page.

CHAPTER FOUR

:

A JOB LOST

In August of 2010 Mom lost her job. She had been with the publishing group from the time that it was a single "Penney Saver" to where it had grown to over 450 newspapers. I think she was with them for about twenty two years. She started as a book keeper and eventually moved up to a district book keeper that managed about 25 others in several other states. For ten or twelve years she traveled at least one week a month, hiring and supervising the other location employees.

For about three weeks she was devastated. She was really upset and I hated to leave her to go to work. She felt like she had failed at her job. She felt like she had let me and her fellow workers down. I tried to assure her that we would be fine financially for a long time and that I knew she would find something else soon.

Finally, one day I came home and found her smiling and in a good mood. I asked her what had changed for her so dramatically. She said, "Today I realized two things. One is that you wouldn't lie to me and I should trust you that we are okay financially for a while. Second, I realized that millions of people have lost their jobs in the last two years, so why shouldn't I? I am not so special that it can't happen to me too." She continued, "I've decided that I can't do anything about losing my job so I'm going to enjoy my time off and make the most of it. I haven't had this much time off in the last 25 years and someday I'll have to go back to work".

I think Megan described the next five months better than I could when she spoke at the funeral. I have added her words on the next page to remind us all of what Mom did during her time off. I have never been more proud of you guys than I was that day. I knew that I could not say anything and certainly didn't want you to feel you had to. But, Megan you gave the best speech ever, under the worst possible conditions. And Matt, when you went up to support her, it took all of my strength to not break down. It was one of those "Mom is smiling in Heaven moments".

This is Megan' s written copy

Peanut, you can do this......Sis, take a deep breath

An amazing Mom. My Girl. The love of my life. My other half. An Angel here and in Heaven. A best friend. A Sister. Big, big Idea Person. MY Confidant. My Rock. Strawberry's Cheryl. Determined. Asks the best Questions. Family. And I could fill hundreds of pages with other descriptions, but the one I know in my heart and the one so many have said, is True believer in her faith and follower of God.

Life changes for anyone can be difficult. We sit here today saying, not goodbye but see ya later to one of God's greatest gifts here on earth...Life changes are what my Mom experienced a few months ago when she lost her job, a place she had worked for over twenty years. The difference, however is what my Mom did after that, in the last few months of her life.

While I'd be lying if I said she wasn't concerned about finding a job and joked about with us how good she was at staying home, she also said that she needed a purpose. She needed a reason to get up and to know that she had responsibility. For all of those that knew her, we already could see what her purpose was as she was living it every day.

In true Mom form, she set out to take care of the world, one person at a time, and then in those last few months multiplied that by ten. And without many of us knowing, she set the stage for all of us to take over her work of taking care of others. I tell you that she has set the bar very high.

In the last few months, she accomplished more than many do in a lifetime. We have heard from many in the last few days that she knew she helped, but also from others that drew peace from her and she probably wasn't even aware.

In these last few months my Mom lived her dream life and while I know for many that vision is different, for my Mom it was being with her family, loving the only man she'd ever loved since they were thirteen, taking care of, laughing, crying and loving from here to there her "other half", best friend, and sister , reconnecting distant families, being as involved as possible with anything and everything to do with her church, celebrating weddings, loving and taking care of children of all ages and looking for opportunities for others. She also re-learned to knit with another starter kit from the same store she bought it from five years ago while volunteering, having coffee, talking with friends and what many of us would call counseling.

She did babysitting, met with friends for lunch, made new friends and started new relationships. She shared her faith with more than I can count and laughed a lot while catching up with those she'd lost touch with over the years. She spent a lot of time cooking and trying new allergy free recipes for me and using my Dad for guinea pig. She asked a lot of interesting questions, reassured others of life's uncertainties and told them that as long as you believe in God everything would be okay. And she developed bigger ideas of how to better the world, like the addition that I guarantee you she's still trying to get built onto the church.

And while these are just a few of the things she worked on, the biggest one she did without even knowing it. She was preparing for what she was most excited about. Going to Heaven and being with God. She wasn't scared, hesitant or nervous about that. She was excited and it was hard not to get excited with her. Whenever God decided it was time and while for very selfish reasons, I'm not ready to say goodbye, I know that without a doubt she's continuing to live the life she always wanted.

So Mom, I love you more than you could ever know, I'm so thankful for you and..........I'll see you later.....

CHAPTER FIVE

:

WORST WEEKEND EVER

On Friday, January 21st, (2011) Mom came down with a headache and upset stomach. There was lots of flu going around so we just thought she needed to get plenty of rest and ride it out. On Saturday, I went to the shop to work but she called about 9:00am and wanted me to come back home. She felt terrible so I convinced her to go to the local clinic. We left home about ten.

After examining Mom, the doctor suspected that she had the flu and that she was very dehydrated. He told her that an anti-biotic would not help but just in case he was sending her for a chest x-ray, urine test and blood test. Honestly, I was upset with the doctor for doing all of those tests when he seemed pretty certain that she had the flu and he wouldn't give her anything for it. It seemed to me that he was just covering himself with a lot of unnecessary tests and I was pretty sure that our new insurance wasn't going to pay for any of it.

After about five hours of tests and a bag of fluid to hydrate her, the doctor told us that all of her tests were negative and that she should go home to rest. The fluids seemed to perk her up and she was hungry so we picked up some chicken nuggets on the way home for her to eat.

Mom slept most of the afternoon and evening while I did bookwork on the veranda. About 8 o'clock she came downstairs and asked if I would fix her something to eat. She ate part of a sandwich and some soup while we visited and watched television. She was feeling much better but said we probably shouldn't go to the football party at her brother's house the next day. She joked that not going to the party did not mean that I had "won." Earlier in the week, we had disagreed about attending the party. I wanted to stay home that Sunday. It seemed like we had hardly seen each other that week. She seemed like the busiest "out of work person" that I knew so I thought it would be nice to spend some time alone together.

About 9:30 Mom said that she was going back to bed and gave me a kiss goodnight. We said we loved each other, as usual, and she took her blanket up to Matt's room. She said she would sleep there because she had developed a cough and didn't want to keep me up.

About 1:00 am. I heard Mom in our upstairs bathroom so went in to check on her. She said that her stomach was upset, her back hurt and she seemed to be coughing more. She returned to our bed but was up off and on through the rest of the night.

By early Sunday morning it was obvious that Mom wasn't well enough to attend church so we kind of settled in the veranda for the day. One of us called her brother or sister and told them we would not be attending the playoff party.

By 9:00 am. I had begun trying to talk Mom into going back to the clinic. I felt she was getting worse and maybe needed an antibiotic or another dose of fluids. She really fought me on going because we had been there the day before and all the tests were okay.

Finally, about 10:00 am. I heard her in the living room coughing and went back to check on her again. She was laying on the floor complaining about her back pain again. She then remarked that she was having trouble breathing. This was the first time that she had said anything about that and it really got my attention. I had read a lot of medical articles about heart attacks and recalled that women often have back pain instead of chest pain. At that time I told her that I was taking her in to the clinic whether she wanted to go or not. With the nausea, the back pain and the trouble breathing I was very worried that she was having a heart attack. I gave her four baby aspirin and got her dressed.

We took off for the hospital at a high rate of speed. On the way there my phone rang but I didn't answer it because I was driving too fast. I did glance at it and saw that it was our pastor. I found out later that he had heard at church that Mom was sick and was calling to check on her.

I pulled up to the emergency room doors and got a wheel chair. I told the lady at the desk that Mom may be having a heart attack. They took her into a room while I gave them the insurance information. (That was probably where our insurance got totally screwed up. I gave them our new numbers but for some reason the bills kept getting put on our old insurance card. It only took about 6 months to get that straightened out!)

Anyway, in the room the doctor asked us a lot of questions. I explained that she had been in the day before (different doctor), the tests were all negative and that she was now complaining about severe back pain and being out of breath. He immediately ordered an EKG. A nurse performed the test and he returned soon after reading it. He said that because of the results he was pretty sure that she wasn't having a heart attack but because of her back pain he wanted to do some kind of a scan. She would need to drink some of that white liquid that tastes like chalk. He ordered that test to be done and went to check on some other patients. The emergency rooms were really filling up by then.

During the next hour two important changes took place. Mom was coughing more and even I could tell that her lungs were filling up. She also complained, even more about her back pain. But, I still wasn't overly concerned. We were in a hospital.

Also, around that time I had called aunt Nan and asked her to bring out some sweats for Mom to change in to when we went home. Nan arrived about the time the nurse realized they were not getting an accurate reading on Mom's blood oxygen content. Her fake nails were too thick for the sensor to work. Nan said that she would run back home to get some acetone to take one of them off. She returned right away and began soaking her fingertips in a bowl. Nan was also trying to get Mom to continue to force down more of the white liquid. While she took care of Mom I was texting with you guys. You kept asking me if you should come home. I still wasn't very worried and we still didn't know what was wrong with her. I think both of you went ahead and left for home even though I hadn't told you to.

I don't remember if Nan ever got one of Mom's nails off or not, or if they ever got an accurate oxygen reading. I do know that they did not actually do the scan. The doctor returned to check on her and after listening to her chest he decided to send her over to a hospital that had a pulmonary specialist on call in Galesburg. (I must add that I was pleased, overall, with the care she received at our local hospital and am very glad that we have it)

They put Mom on the ambulance cart and got the fluids and oxygen set up so that she could continue to receive them on her short trip there (about 15 minutes). As we were about to leave our pastor and his wife came to the room. They talked to us both and told me to keep them posted. Aunt Nan and I decided to drive there separately. She left first while I waited for them to leave with Mom.

I know this sounds crazy now but I still wasn't terribly worried at that time. So many things had happened so fast that I think that I just hadn't caught up with what was actually going on. I still thought that she just had a bad case of the flu and the dr. hadn't told me any different.

I think you guys had already taken off by the time we moved Mom to Galesburg. I don't remember being at that hospital very long before you showed up there. I had talked to Grandma earlier the day before and she just happened to call to check on Mom as I was driving to the next hospital. I don't remember exactly what I said to her, but apparently the way I responded was enough to get her attention. She must have told Grandpa immediately after our conversation that they were going to come home (they were in Arizona). I think it was when I was actually telling Grandma about Mom's condition that it finally struck me that whatever Mom had was serious.

When I got to the hospital I went to the admissions desk to get Mom checked in. They told me that she was up in the ICU. Nan was already up there and was talking to the head nurse (they knew each other).

The nurse said that they were working on Mom and the pulmonary doctor was on the way to the hospital. She thought that he would probably want to intubate her to improve her breathing. He arrived soon and after examining her told me that he didn't think that tubing Mom was necessary because she seemed to be responding to the oxygen mask they had placed on her. They could tell her oxygen stats had come up because they had put a sensor on her toe. (That's why I'm not sure anyone ever got her fake nail off) Anyway, this conversation with the doctor made me feel better and I thought we were finally getting this thing under control. I was in the room talking to her and telling her to not fight the oxygen mask. It actually forced air into her lungs each time that she breathed in. I stayed in with her until someone told me that you guys were outside and I went to see you. It was then that I discovered that most of Mom's family (brothers and their wives), my cousin and his wife and our pastor and his wife were there also.

As you know, Mom's condition deteriorated quickly, soon after. They called the doctor back and he did decide to go ahead and intubate her to help her breathing. While he had her under for that he also told me he would "scope" her lungs so he could actually see what was going on with them. He was still trying to figure out just what was working on her so hard. Before the procedure I quickly gave her a kiss, told her I loved her and said that I would see her when she woke up. (I could tell the nurses wanted me to hurry. There was a definite urgency to what they were doing.)

The doctor came out to speak to us when he was done. I think the procedure took about 45 minutes. He said that when he looked at her lungs he found they were full of blood. The infection seemed to be moving through them quickly and they were hardly working. The machine was doing the breathing for her. He said that we should be prepared for a long night.

I think I knew then that the situation wasn't going to turn out well. They had been pumping three different antibiotics into Mom and none of them seemed to be helping. I had never seen something attack a healthy person so quickly.

I really hadn't said anything but quick prayers during the day. I was just making decisions as each new phase came up and listening to doctors but really had no time to myself to really think about what was happening. I went out in the hallway to pray and gather my courage for what I felt was to come.

I was not there very long before a nurse came to get me. She said things were moving fast, in the wrong direction so I should stay close. As I remember, you and your spouses, three of Mom's brothers and their wives, and aunt Nan were with me in the room. There were also two nurses and eventually the dr. came in also. Shortly after we all got in there her heart stopped and several buzzers went off on the monitors. It lasted for about thirty seconds but then her heart started beating again. The older nurse looked at me and told me what had happened. She said that they needed to know if I wanted them to try extraordinary measures if her heart stopped again but didn't restart on its own.

It was then that I asked the doctor if her lungs were working at all and if they ever would. He quickly replied that not only were they not working but that something was attacking them at an alarming rate. I then asked if her kidneys were working. He replied that they had stopped working about two hours before. He also added that their efforts had not even slowed down whatever was attacking her internal organs and that he didn't believe Mom could live in her condition. (We found out later she had a severe infection called "strep a".)

About three or four minutes later, her heart stopped again, but did not restart. The older nurse asked me again what I wanted them to do. She was hooked up to a ventilator, Iv's and various other machines. None of it had slowed down the infection. I felt then that I had already lost her, that her spirit was gone. I just no longer felt her presence in the room and at that time, had no doubt about what I had to do. I told the doctor and the nurses to "let her go".

I feel so very lucky that there were no family members trying to tell me what to do at that time. I somehow knew in my heart that Mom was already gone. I also knew where she was and who she was with. She was where she wanted to be. She had died while surrounded by people that loved her and went quickly without pain.

I may not have the exact order of events or the correct arrival of some people but this is the way I remember that day. I know there were lots of people praying for Mom that night but I don't know who called for our church prayer chain to be activated. I left the hospital in total shock of what happened and really stayed that way for the next several months. I remember hugging Megan in the hallway and saying, "I brought Mom in for the flu but I'm not taking her home". That was Monday, January 24th at 12.25 am. She was just 54 years old.

There are a lot of "what ifs" that I could dwell on concerning Mom's death. What if the doctor on the first visit to the clinic had given her an antibiotic, as a preventative? Doctors do that all the time. Why not this time? What if Mom did not have the fake nails? Would the drop in her blood oxygen content have been responded to sooner? What if I had taken her to the hospital sooner? There's really no end to these questions. I've spent a lot of time thinking about the answers and what happened that day and come to this conclusion. The events of that day happened for a reason. God's reason.

A friend of Mom's that she worked with for over twenty years, sent me an e-mail about one month after Mom died. In it she explained that when her sister died, Mom was very supportive of her, long after others quit asking her how she was doing. They were eating lunch one day and the friend was beating herself up over not forcing her sister to go see a doctor sooner. She stated that Mom looked at her from across the table and said, "It wouldn't have mattered. The Bible says that when it is your time, there is nothing you or anyone can do to stop it. It was your sister's time so stop worrying about it. Nothing you would have done could change that."

I take a huge amount of peace away from that story. I truly need to tell Mom's friend how much I needed to hear it that day. (I finally did tell her but almost 4 years later) I am very grateful that she passed it on to me and feel that was Mom's way of letting me know that I made the right decisions that day.

We all went to sleep that night in the beds that we had slept in for years. Except, I slept alone. I had obviously slept alone before, as Mom traveled the country for her job. But, I always knew that she would be home soon. This was definitely different and something that is still hard to do. (To this day I can only sleep with lots of pillows in the bed so it feels like someone is sleeping with me. I also have never slept on "her side". It just doesn't feel right to me and I have talked to several other widowers that feel the same.)

I had only slept about three hours the night before and it was already 2:30 am then. About four o'clock I got up and sat in the bathroom crying and wondering how I was going to handle the next few days. I could not see any further than that and still don't look very far ahead. It was at that time that I wrote the words that we eventually put on the back of the funeral bulletin. I didn't have any paper and didn't want to wake up anyone by going downstairs so I scribbled it on the back of an old envelope.(I still have it) I wasn't writing it with the intent of anyone seeing it. I simply felt that way at that time and wanted to write it down so I wouldn't forget it. (That may have been the beginnings of this book.) The words that Megan e-mailed to our pastor are on the next page.

This is for the back of the bulletin

The Earth stood still today and I don't know if I can get it started,

Water stopped flowing,

Engines quit turning,

Dogs stopped barking,

Plants stopped growing.

Children stopped yelling,

The wind stopped blowing.

And maybe the worst part of all, the Earth stopped making a sound.

The Earth stood still today, and without You, I may never get it started.

Bear

CHAPTER SIX

:

YOU SHALL EAT!

About six am I heard noise downstairs so I went down to see who was up. (I'd had about 5 hours of sleep in the last two nights) I found Megan cleaning the kitchen. She said, "Dad, you don't have very much food around so we'll need to go to the grocery store this morning." I just smiled and said, "Honey, you don't realize what is about to happen. When ladies of the community hear what has happened, food will appear. There will be so much food by tonight that we'd better clean out the refrigerator in the garage to make room for it all." I was wrong. By that night, both refrigerators were full and so were both freezers. The next day we started filling up coolers in the garage and outside the back door!

Sometime that day, we realized we needed a way to keep track of it all so we could be sure to thank people later. By evening Megan had started a spreadsheet on her computer.

The outpouring of support was unbelievable. So many called, sent cards, reached out on-line and came by the house that it was truly overwhelming. Members of our families, people in our community, our church family and literally people from all over the country that Mom had worked with, expressed their sympathy. I really didn't realize that we knew that many people or that they cared that much. Mom touched a lot of people. She gave them so much of herself and her time.

I think I still have pies and cakes in my freezer left over from that week. Even after all this time they are probably still better than anything you could buy at the grocery store. When something bad happens, you can count on country folks to take care of the food. It's a fact.

CHAPTER SEVEN

:

FUNERAL DECISIONS

One of the things that really surprised me, that Monday morning, was how quickly people started wanting me to make decisions. At 7 am I received a call from the funeral home wanting us to come in and set up the funeral. We had just arrived home about 2:30 am so it kind of caught me off guard. Mom and I had discussed our funeral arrangements over the years and actually just a few months earlier. I just didn't realize how quickly I would have to finalize the plans.

We already had our cemetery plot purchased, probably because Grandpa and I are on the local cemetery board. Otherwise, like a lot of people, we may had not thought about that yet. (There is room for 8 burials in a plot) I had always joked that I was going to be buried at an angle in the plot so that I would be overlooking the bottom ground across the road. I said I wanted to be able to watch the poor guy that has to try and raise a crop down there after I'm gone. We have many relatives buried in that cemetery (Belmont) dating back to the first Morris who made a living on our farm. I am the 6th generation to live in the house and farm it and you guys are 7th since 1856.

Mom and I spent quite a bit of time discussing where to hold our funerals. We had never thought about having them at the church until a friend of ours held her husband's there. We just felt that it was very fitting, after that one, to have your funeral where you worship every Sunday. (most of the funerals that we had attended until then were held at a funeral home) It was also very important to us to have our "church family" there.

Mom had also made it very clear to all of us that she wanted to be cremated. She knew that it was cheaper to be cremated. She always said, "Why spend the money on a funeral? You are already in Heaven or Hell by then."

She felt the same way about gravestones. I found that you can spend $2000 to $50,000 on a stone. I tried to be conservative about what I picked out. I knew that she would rather have a wooden cross and give the rest of the money to someone who really needed it. (No, it's not wood but it is simple and traditional)

I truly believed that we should celebrate Mom's life at the funeral. She was such a positive person that the service needed to show her love of God and her church family. She was always such a big supporter of the church praise band that I just knew that we had to have them play. I chose, "Awesome is the Lord Most High" by Chris Tomlin because it was one of her favorites and I think Matt asked for "Amazing Grace." I am sure it was quite a shock to some of those attending the funeral when the drummer started pounding on the drums! Another "Mom is Dancing Heaven" moment.

The rest of the service had two things that were important to Mom and I. Our pastor preached the gospel of Jesus Christ to all of us there. He always says that if a non-member wants him to speak at their funeral they are gonna get the "message" whether they want it or not. Of course, Mom was member and we wanted to hear it.

The other part of the service that was so important was the speech given by Megan and the poem read by Mom's niece. I was never more proud of you than when you gave that speech, Megan. I was also very proud of you Matt for going up to support her. As I have said, a moment I will never forget. (On the next page is the speech that my brother(Tom) wrote but we somehow managed to exclude.)

TRIBUTE TO CHERYL

As I think back of all the great memories of times spent with Cheryl and Barry, one thing keeps coming to mind. Whenever you were with Cheryl, it was never about Cheryl. It was always about you or someone else. Cheryl truly was a woman with the heart of a servant. A servant of the Lord. She always wanted to do something for someone else, with absolutely no need of recognition. She wanted it that way. And if a little bit of something was good, then a lot was even better. She cared about Barry and Megan and Matt, and in time Bob and Candace as if they were her own. She cared for everyone who crossed her path. Family or friend or coworker or stranger. It mattered not to her. She cared for them all and wanted to help. No questions asked. She had the unique ability to not judge people and see the good in everyone she met.

I recall a conversation I had with Barry when he called to tell me that Cheryl had lost her job at the newspaper after 22 years. He knew that I had gone through something similar the year before. He asked me if I would call and talk to her because she was struggling somewhat, to deal with the reality of being out of work after she had dedicated herself to her job for all those years. I called her a day or two later and we talked for 30-40 minutes. It was a good talk. I assured her that things would work out, that hopefully she would find a job soon. And as always she made me feel better as we talked, despite the fact it was supposed to be me helping her. Little did any of us know that she was already in a perfect place, doing the perfect thing she was called to do......quit working for the newspaper and get busy with her fulltime job of doing the Lord's work in this community. After the initial shock of losing her job had worn off, it appears to me that Cheryl, knowingly or unknowingly, guided by a higher power, jumped head on into her next position. It was one she had been training for all of her life. She was a full time servant of doing God's work, unpaid and loving it.

Cheryl was never about Cheryl. She worked hard for others. She never said No to anyone. She took on more than you would think could possibly be done. She was tireless in nearly everything she did. Whether she was wrapping Christmas presents at three in the morning(every year), cooking more food than anyone could possibly consume in a day, calling on others, seeing to the needs of family and neighbors and friends and even strangers who were about to be her friend....she always made it work. As many of you already know, she gave the best hugs in the world. When Cheryl hugged you , you knew you had been hugged. She gave them out freely and gave every one with feeling. She loved Barry. She loved her kids. She loved her friends. She loved her God. She loved her church and she loved life. We loved her and will miss her greatly. We find peace in knowing she is exactly where she hoped to be some day.

Save me a place Cheryl. We love you.

Uncle Tom

MEGAN READ THIS, FOR ME AT CHURCH

THE SUNDAY AFTER MOM DIED

(I WAS HOME SICK WITH A SINUS INFECTION AND A

FEVER)

TO OUR CHURCH FAMILY,

The loss of Cheryl last week has left a hole in our hearts that we may never be able to fill. She defined who we were as a team and my team is now incomplete, but with your help we hope to carry on.

We have been so overwhelmed at the outpouring of love and support from this church, our community and from all over the United States. No matter where she worked she seemed to have touched someone. I've always known she was special. I just never realized, until now, how many other people thought so also.

We cannot begin to name each individual who contributed to the celebration of Cheryl's life but we want you to know that we have been humbled at what you all have done to make this easier on us and a tribute to Cher. She was watching us from above this week, full of joy and proud to tell Jesus, "Yes, that's my church family." Please keep us in your prayers.

BARRY, MEGAN, MATT, BOB and CANDACE

At this time I would also like to tell you how proud I am of my other "kids". Candace (Matt's wife), your love and support of Matt, and all of us, is something I will always remember. Especially during that first week. The night that you, your mom, and your aunt organized my kitchen really stands out for me. It was a mess with stacks of food, dishes, coolers etc. taking over and growing fast. I felt like I should come in and help in some way as you gals went about the task of getting it straightened up. But your Uncle assured me that I should stay out of the way. He'd seen that crew at work many times before. And he was right. I stayed out and my kitchen became spotless and organized in no time. Not the most important issue for some, maybe. But for me, who felt like he had lost all control of his life, well, to me it was a big deal. Again, thank you for being there for all of us when we really needed you.

And then there's Bob(Megan's husband) I am sure that I was not even remotely aware of all the things you were doing to help out, especially with Megan. Grandpa actually started calling you "Super Bob" behind your back. He told me later that you were just always hanging around looking for something to help with. Being named "Super Bob" by grandpa is quite an achievement. Thank you!

Another decision we had to make right away was what to have Mom's memorial money go to. The funeral home likes to have something to put in the newspaper with the arrangements so people know what they are donating to. I knew it should have something to do with the youth and missions of the church but there just wasn't the right fund to put the money in at that time. I believe it was our pastor who suggested we simply open an account in Mom's name at the bank. This gave us time to think about how we really wanted to use it. Since then we have donated to the church mission trips, the Easter Egg Hunt, the Thanksgiving Lunch and the Blessings in a Backpack program. All of these events had a special place in Mom's heart.

Since Mom was being cremated I didn't think that we would need pallbearers at the funeral. But then I realized we needed ushers at the church and help in moving the casket around in the church. (She wasn't cremated until after the funeral) I chose these guys based on two things. First, I wanted men who attended our church and worked with Mom on various projects there. There were, as it turned out, many who fit this description because of her many projects. This made it hard to get the list down to what we actually needed. Looking back, I left off people who I should have asked. It's hard to get everything just right when you are making so many decisions at once.

I should also add at this time that the funeral home did a great job of handling Mom's funeral and visitation. They told me afterward that they were prepared for a large crowd at the visitation but had no idea it would be that big. They said that up until then, it was the largest crowd they had ever had through their building (800 +) and it was the largest crowd anyone could ever remember being in our church. I felt so proud of the ushers that made that happen.

At this time I would like to document how it came to be that Mom's grave was dug by hand. After the visitation one of the employees came to me and asked to have a word with me. He said that he had received a call from a friend of mine stating that he would like to dig Mom's grave. (It was near the end of January and the ground was frozen down about 12 inches) The employee said that he had never had such a request and that he didn't want to offend him. He wanted to know if I would like to talk to him and tell him that someone else was lined up to dig the grave with a "back hoe". I quickly said that he should call my friend back and tell him that I would be honored if he would like to dig the grave. The employee just shook his head and went back to the office to make the call.

My friend had been with me the week before when I had to go to the cemetery to mark a grave for someone. While there we had discussed how graves used to be dug by hand. My friend felt that was the way it should still be done. In his grief, at my loss, he wanted to do something for me. It was greatly appreciated and I will never forget the gesture. As you know, later that summer he and I had to dig the urn back up and move it as there was a mix up on our gravestone lettering so it was on the wrong side. Not wanting you guys to have to deal with it later and after notifying the other board members, we moved Mom's ashes to the correct side.

I also asked this friend to take my tractor and blade over to the cemetery and clean a path to the grave site before the graveside service (We had a lot of snow on the ground.) I found out later that he was worried about tearing up the grass so he scooped most of the path with a shovel. I will never forget these acts of kindness.

I will also never forget coming home from the funeral home after making the arrangements. The gravel roads were snow packed and very slick when we left for town. But when we returned two hours later, the road was much safer. As soon as we left the pavement, we noticed that someone had spread sand on the ice all the way to my house (about 2.0 miles.) Another gesture that was totally unexpected.

These are just a couple of the many things that our family and friends stepped in to help us with. There were many, many more since then and they are still helping to this day. I cannot write about them all but wanted you to know of these particular examples. They represent the not so little things that people did for us when we were really in need.

CHAPTER EIGHT

:

FUNERAL DINNER

First of all, in the country we have dinner around noon. Not lunch. To have one or not? Where to have it? Who should attend? What to serve? I will never forget the discussions about this important feature of all rural funerals. Once again, when we are stressed, we eat. The church ladies make sure of that.

As we all know, at least in our part of the country, there is someone at every church in charge of "dinners". At our church, at that point in time, it happened to be my aunt. For the last twenty years, maybe longer, she was the person to talk to if you wanted or needed a church dinner. For the last ten years several of us guys "got" to help set up the chairs and tables in preparation for all dinners. I learned the routine very well. Better than I ever thought I would. Over time I learned that you can't just go putting tables and chairs out randomly. They have a particular place that they must be set up and it seemed like we guys struggled with remembering the proper protocol.

Anyway, I assumed that my aunt would take care of the dinner. So, when she came to my house on the day after Mom died, bearing food and offering her sympathies, I figured I had better talk to her about it. I ran into her in the kitchen and told her that I would be needing to discuss the dinner arrangements. As you know, she could be pretty tough. Especially when it came to handling church dinners the "correct way." So you can imagine my surprise when she looked at me and said, "I can't do this one Barry. I just can't." Tears came to her eyes as she repeated, "I just can't do this one for Cheryl. It's too hard." I'm sure my jaw dropped as I struggled with the words to respond.

She finally spoke again and said that she had asked her granddaughter who was also on the "dinner committee" to be in charge. That was probably the most emotion I had ever seen come from my aunt and I will never forget it. Sometimes we are surprised at who we touched while here on earth. Sometimes we don't know who that is until we are gone.

(The dinner was great and her granddaughter, along with a lot of help from our church family, did a wonderful job)

CHAPTER NINE

:

I AM LOST

The rest of this book will be devoted to explaining what it's been like for me to lose Mom and some of the effects it's had on my life. Some of the things I anticipated. Many, I did not. I once described how I felt the first couple of months after Mom died like this, "It's like having a panic attack, all day, every day. I feel so anxious but I really don't know why." Some of you told me that was a description of how you felt also. I'm not complaining. I just want you to have some understanding of how much my life has changed. It may help explain why I do some of the things I do.

Probably, the biggest change in my life is my attitude, the way I look at everyday living. Mom and I were a team that depended very heavily on each other. When I was down and overloaded at work, she picked up the pieces and vice versa. I always knew early in life what I wanted and where I thought I was headed. Now, I often feel like I'm just aimlessly wondering through life, letting it control me. (That's what I used to say about Mom and shopping.

She just wondered aimlessly.) Everything I do now is based on what is right in front of me. I have no long term plans. I don't mean that from a religious point of view. That hasn't changed. If anything, events have reinforced my ideas about God and Heaven. What I'm not sure about is my life here on earth. And more specifically, my social life.

Losing Mom really kicked my confidence in social settings. It's taken a long time for me to get most of that back, but it still sneaks up on me sometimes when I'm not ready for it. I think that's why I get a little nervous when I leave home. At home I know where I stand and I'm surrounded by Mom's things and memories of how it used to be. I'm getting better at "living alone" but it's still definitely something I have to work at. I have never been single or even thought of myself as single since high school. But that is what I am now. I didn't even realize that until I had to fill out a new W-4 tax form for the township road commissioner's job. The supervisor sort of choked up when she pointed out that I needed to change my status. Even now, over a year later, I am still trying to figure out where I fit and where I am headed. I feel like I am gaining but after 35 years of being on a team, it is really hard to think as one person. You guys do the same thing as I did but probably don't even realize it. When someone asks you to go somewhere or if you want to do something, your answer is based on your experience of knowing what you and your spouse would want to do. That's the way you are supposed to think after you get married. I once made the statement that I was afraid I would get used to being alone all the time. That really does worry me. I just haven't figured out why or what to do about it yet.

CHAPTER TEN

:

SOCIAL EVENTS

Regular social events are a problem. It doesn't matter if it's going out to dinner or going to church on Sunday. I told Megan, early on, that one of my biggest worries was not knowing where to sit at church. Obviously, there are no reserved or assigned seats at church but, if you pay attention you will see that people have a tendency to sit in the same place most of the time. Megan never told me, but I am sure that she must have voiced my concerns to at least two couples at church about my dilemma. They have made it a point to ask me to sit with them every Sunday. This has been unbelievably helpful. I just felt so uncomfortable and out of place. I may have actually stopped going if I hadn't have had help on this. I know it's silly but it's surprising what bothers you after your world is turned upside down. It's the little things. Seriously. Mom and I always attended social events together. Business meetings were okay to show up at alone but show up at a church potluck without your spouse and see how many notice.

Speaking of potlucks, I am not a cook. This is also a problem. So far, I have only attended potlucks that Grandma is attending also. She always says that she will take enough food to "cover" me. I don't know how long I can milk that but it's still working for me now.

Of course I attend social events other than those at church. I find that when I am stressed about attending one, there are two sets of people that can make me feel at ease. First, I can attend any event that you kids are also going to. I always feel comfortable when you are around. I also feel comfortable around family and old friends, as long as it isn't a very large crowd. But put me in a group of people I barely know and I am gonna have problems.

I have had many, many friends helping me in many ways. I have grown to rely on them and don't really know how I could ever repay them. I hope that one day I can be as helpful to them as they have been to me.

CHAPTER ELEVEN

:

CHURCH GREETER

Being a church greeter is another issue for a single person. There are always two people to greet folks and to take up the collection on Sunday morning. Recently, this has become a problem for me. Until now, I have only been a greeter if you kids were home to help me or if someone needs me to fill in for them.

Do I greet with another single man? Do I greet with a single lady who happens to be a friend? (that usually is good for keeping the rumor mill filled for a while) Or do I get some large family to adopt me and hope no one notices? This is one of the mysteries that I have failed to work out at this time. For now, I have just told the person in charge of such things to take me off the greeter list.

CHAPTER TWELVE

:

GROCERIES AND COOKING

Potlucks aren't the only time it would help if I could cook. (I actually can cook a little but find that it takes away from my time to eat) It seems that I like to eat almost every day. This requires that there be food in my refrigerator and in my cupboards. (Well, on top of my counters is actually about as far as it gets) Which brings us to grocery shopping. Let's be honest here. I like, most folks I know, hate to shop for groceries. Therefore, early on, I came up with a plan to make grocery shopping tolerable. I've made it a competitive sport! Me against the clock. I'm allowed thirteen minutes to finish, which is about the minimum, for a normal "run". If I am not finished in that time, according to the rules, I must leave anyway and come back another day. I don't want to come back the next day! It is on my schedule for today and I live 20 miles from the store. So, I must win. The only thing that allows me to go over time is if I run into a friend who wants to visit. Then I am allotted another three minutes. Running into two friends in one trip is a problem. I try to avoid the "second encounter" at all costs. Therefore shopping at ten pm. on Saturday night is a good time to shop. Except for one problem, they are usually out of fried chicken at ten pm! Later, in this chapter you will find out why this forces me to go earlier.

I find that only about 60 percent of what I buy at the grocery store is food. The rest is stuff like toilet paper, shampoo, toothpaste etc. I've found that I can buy about 85% of the 60% already cooked, processed or sorted for me. That 85% of the 60% is what I am after. I only eat a banana and coffee at home for breakfast and hardly ever eat lunch at home so I am mostly shopping for supper. I eat out about three nights a week so I am really only shopping for four supper meals, coffee and bananas. There are 21 meals a week so if I only eat at home for 4 of them it's only about 20%. No problem. Buying the same thing all the time also helps on the 13 minute rule. It's a finely tuned system. Try to keep up here!

In school they teach us that we need meat, vegetables fruit and a little starch each meal. I've got that covered. I get green beans or spinach in a can and eat half the can one night and the other half the next. Both are dark green so I figure I'm getting the maximum vegetable benefits from them.

I buy fruit cups to cover the fruit requirement. I don't like fruit any better than I like vegetables so I get the mixed fruit to cover all the bases. It keeps Megan from harassing me also. Tator salad covers your starches on the food wheel. Both delis where I shop have great tator salad already made. They must have taken "Great Tator Salad Class" in cooking school.

Finally, we get to the main ingredient of my supper meals, fried chicken. Who doesn't like fried chicken? (I must admit that sometimes they have pulled pork and steamed hamburger at the deli also and I go clear "out of the box" and eat those for a change) All meats must meet the two requirements though. Purchasing the "other" meats must not cause me to fall behind my 13 minute schedule. And they must be processed enough that they do not mess up the other all- important requirement. Cooking my supper must not take more than one minute and 30 seconds in the microwave. I don't like cooking any more than I like shopping so I only allow about 9% of the time it takes to shop, for cooking. Still with me?

These rules have been developed over time and are finely tuned. I intend to pass them down to my grandchildren in a super, double secret text. Although, I've also thought about writing a book based solely on the one minute and thirty second meal. I am confident it would be an instant best seller with single guys, soccer moms and people in New York City. (I have never been to New York but I hear that life moves really fast there) It would not be popular with country folks. I know that for a fact. Because I have offered to bring meals to some of my friends and for some reason they have refused. They probably wouldn't buy my book then. But it would still be a mega hit. Just do the math. Only 3% of the population are farmers. That means that 97% of the 300+ million people in this country would still love my book. I'm gonna be rich! It will be three pages long, with the table of contents and a foreword by Rachael Ray. (I'm sure she wants in on this) Four pages if I include a picture of my meal in the micro wave. I could take the picture with the smarty phone that I'm gonna buy with all my book money!

Anyway, it would be a mistake if I didn't talk about the importance of the local café to my good health. I eat there at least five meals a week. It's good food. It's clean and the women spoil me. I know this has to be true because they tell me that every day. It's kind of like Norm walking into "Cheers". Everyone knows your name. When you eat most of your meals alone, it's a nice break to have adult conversation during some of them.

All over America there are small cafes like the one I eat at. They are run by hardworking people just trying to make a living, feeding people like me. I have a lot of respect for people like that. I am a loyal customer and a good tipper. (Well, I at least give them plenty of tips.)

CHAPTER THIRTEEN

:

IT'S BUSINESS

Mom and I did have wills. They were very old but I guess they worked just fine. We did not have power of attorneys for financial or medical. Looking back, I'm actually surprised that no one at the hospital ever asked me for a medical POA considering the decisions I had to make. Because we owned almost everything together and our wills said the surviving spouse received everything, Mom's estate was settled easily. It did not have to go through the probate process first. All of our bank accounts, the house deed, farm and business loans and car and truck loans were held and signed by both of us. All of these things have been placed strictly in my name now with no real problems. (We had no life insurance on Mom because it was with her old company and she lost it when she was let go. I didn't think there was any hurry in replacing it as I was certain that I would die first and we had plenty on me. Actually, just two months before she died our insurance agent and Mom tried to get me to take out a policy on her. I thought we could wait until she got another job and get it there.) But, there were some things that took some time and patience on my part to get straightened out.

Probably my biggest fear about our finances was in paying the personal bills. In thirty five years I had never paid any of them. I always took care of the business bills and Mom paid the personal ones. My system was simple. Bills would come in the mail and I would send them a check for the amount due. I had told Mom many times in the previous year that I would be in so much trouble if anything ever happened to her. She would just laugh and say, "Oh, you'll figure it out."

Of course the problem was that she had almost every personal bill deducted automatically or she paid them on line. With several different pay services. Not one. Four. We think. It took you guys three months to get all of the things stopped and get me back on paper statements. All but one bill. We never did figure out how to stop the long distance phone bill from being drafted out of my account. I think you guys just gave up. Mom would think that's funny. I, on the other hand needed a paper bag to breath into whenever I just thought of someone being able to take money out of my account without my permission. That has improved a lot but I'm sweating now just telling you about it. I think that falls into the category of me not having control of my life again.

Mom and I each had a retirement account. The will, of course said that I was to receive hers in the event of her passing first. It was still at her old employers. In New York. First, I had to prove that Mom had actually passed. Not as easy as you would think. When the funeral home offers to get you several death certificates, do not turn them down. Get a bunch. You will need them. I also found out that you will need several official copies of your wills.

It took six weeks to get Mom's former company to release her 401k. I made several trips to our lawyer, the court house, the bank and the accountants. It wasn't that I was going to spend it any time soon but it made me nervous that the same people who fired her had her money. Eventually, I got the balance transferred here except for the $140.00 that the account made while the process was taking place.(stocks happened to be in a rally at the time) And yes, they wanted me to go through the whole process again to release that money. I recently found out that there was some actual stock involved in that balance. I have been able to get that stock placed in my name but haven't been through the process of actually disposing of it yet. I just got tired of fighting with them. So, I just decided to let them send me statements for the rest of my life to punish them for making everything so hard. It's the principle, right? Good luck in straightening that mess out after I'm gone.

Mom and I had stopped using all but one credit card before she had passed. It was her attempt at trying to do a better job at managing our money. I continued to use that card after she had passed. I paid it off every month. I saw no reason to change anything as I had cut up her card and just used mine. For about 14 months everything worked just fine. Until the card reached its expiration date and it was time to renew it. The company sent me two new cards. I called to activate mine and to cancel Mom's card. Big mistake. Being honest created another mess. The person to whom I was speaking practically gasped in the phone when I told her that Mom had died so they didn't need to issue her another card. She said that I didn't have the right to use the old card because I was not the primary card holder. She said that she was canceling my card immediately and that I would have to apply for a new card. And that I was not even responsible for whatever balance was on the card currently. I tried to assure her that I was married to the primary card holder for 35 years and that I fully intended to pay for anything that I had used it to buy. If she would just send me the bill! Instead they sent me some forms to fill out. And she transferred me to two other people who also chewed me out for using the card and took more information for their records. My old card had a $20,000 limit on it after being with them for twenty some years. My new one has a $2500 limit. They still won't let me pay the old one off. I guess I should have bought a new car.

About 5 years before Mom died I wrote out directions for her on where I did business and how to dissolve the business if something were to happen to me. I named people who I trusted and that I thought would be helpful to her. (I, of course was certain that I would die first and I also knew she really didn't pay much attention to the business side of the farm) I also listed my life insurance policies and who to contact about them. We had already purchased our burial plots and had discussed our funeral plans.

I thought I was prepared. I had everything covered. Except, I was to die first. It really hasn't worked out like I thought it would. I hope you guys have wills and POA"s for medical and financial and have discussed your funeral plans and wishes. It will certainly relieve your spouse of some of their worries if the unthinkable happens.

CHAPTER FOURTEEN

:

HOUSE CLEANING

Back when Mom traveled a lot for her job and worked a lot of hours we decided it would be helpful to have someone come in and catch up on the cleaning once in a while. Of course we stopped that service when she lost her job. After Mom passed away, I decided to ask our previous cleaning lady (who is also a neighbor and a friend of ours) if she could come by occasionally and take care of the things that I wasn't. Believe it or not, I really don't make a big mess of the house. But, I also did not want our house to become a college bachelor pad. More importantly, I did not want you guys coming home and feeling like you needed to clean while you are here. We don't get a lot of time together so I didn't want you to spend our time cleaning my house. Besides, it gives my cleaning lady an excuse to rearrange my stuff. So Megan has more time to dispose of the outdated food in my cupboards and refrigerator when she is here. And to put things back where they always were. That way my stuff doesn't get stale because it's always moving.

CHAPTER FIFTEEN

:

STUFF

At this writing I have not disposed of any of Mom's "stuff". Her clothes, makeup and jewelry are still here where she left them. It gives me comfort to have her things in my house. Eventually, I will have to get a lot of her stuff moved out. For now, I have just put her clothes in my closet. I know people who immediately got rid of anything that had to do with their spouse. I think it will be a while before I can ever do that. For each of us widowers it is different. There is no one way that works for all of us. More likely, I will eventually pass most of it on to you guys and the rest will just stay with me forever. Just like Mom.

CHAPTER SIXTEEN

:

THE RING AND THE STONE

On December 21st, 1975 Mom and I were married. In a church, in front of God and our families. We declared our love for each other and our devotion until "death do us part". And we gave each other rings to wear so that people would know that we were already committed to someone. After Mom died I could not take off my wedding ring. For thirty five years, whenever I wasn't working I wore my ring. I remember talking to the guys, (Matt and Bob) one night while we sat around the fire pit in the backyard of the house we were staying at. I told them that I felt people who knew that I had lost Mom were looking at it and wandering why I still had it on. But I still felt married to Mom. Another dilemma that I wasn't prepared for. I finally told them that night that I thought I would wear it for at least a year after she died and then try going without it. Which I have done. But I look at it every time I go out and feel I should have it on.

I also encountered another problem that I hadn't anticipated. I had a gravestone placed on our plot after we buried Mom's ashes there. (I already mentioned that the names were on the wrong side so we had to move her ashes.)Under our names are our children's names and dates of birth. This all makes sense, right? Well, it did to me until a friend and I were over at the cemetery watering the new grass around the gravestone. I don't know why but it hit me that I (and every other widower) could potentially have a big problem someday. What if I got re-married? I had just never thought about how that would be handled. I already have Mom's and my names on the stone. Where would I be buried? What about my new wife's name? What about her former spouse? Would we need a whole new plot with a different gravestone? (Don't worry I'm not planning on getting re-married anytime soon. That's not the point.) The point is that losing your spouse, especially at such an early age screws up almost every aspect of your life. We started out with this perfect plan of how we wanted our life to go. You guys are married so you know what I'm talking about. But life very seldom goes as planned. Ever. Some things are better and some things are definitely worse than you thought. I go home to an empty house every night in the middle of a cornfield. I really hope that I don't get used to this.

Mom and I had recently discussed what we would do if the other one passed away. (She tended to bring up all sorts of unwanted discussions and insisted on answers.) As I told you, I said that I would probably sit in the veranda in my recliner and watch television if something happened to her. I cannot replace Mom. Ever. But I would not mind having someone to hang out with. Please don't be upset that I have told you this. I know it's the first time that I have even mentioned it. But if we can't be honest with each other, then this just isn't going to work.

CHAPTER SEVENTEEN

:

HOUSE DECORATING

As you know, Mom was a fan of color. I guess I am too but maybe a little less extreme color. (Remember the bright pink ceiling in the dining room and the loud purple in Megan's bedroom?) I usually did all of the wallpapering, painting and laid the flooring but Mom picked them out. Although at times I refused to continue until she came home after work and saw what it was actually going to look like. Pillow cases, sheets bedspreads and curtains were not really in my department either. But now I am learning all about these things. My first try at picking out paint for my first post Mom project ended when I screamed at aunt Nan on the phone one night that, "I just want something white!" I did not know that Lowes had 36 shades of white paint.

Anyway the room looks nice, if I do say so myself, and I am especially proud of covering up the "power purple" that Mom insisted on putting in Megan's bedroom. At least I'm not letting the house fall apart or turning it into a "man cave". I'm pretty sure you won't let me do that.

CHAPTER EIGHTEEN

:

VACATIONS

Our family started taking a short vacation together about five years ago. Of course Mom was the instigator. She was also the one who made family time so much fun. Her passion for spending unrushed time with us was hard to say no to. So far we have continued this tradition, but I don't want you to feel we have to. Don't take that wrong. I also really enjoy that time because we all make an effort to leave work at home. Just hanging out with absolutely nothing planned or scheduled is what allows us to listen to each other instead of just talking. But I also know you need time away from work for yourselves. Heck, I might just take off on my own. Where would I go? I have no idea but it might be interesting to see where I would end up!

As far as vacations are concerned I want you to remember one thing. It doesn't matter where we go as long as we make an effort to actually engage in meaningful conversation. Put down the phones for a little while and see if you can learn something new about your brother, sister, brother-in-law, sister-in law or Dad. That's what makes our trips worthwhile. It's also why Mom asked such silly questions on our trips. She simply wanted us to come away with a better understanding of what each of us go through in our daily lives. Her questions were just meant to be the catalyst that started the conversations. And that they did.

CHAPTER NINETEEN

:

MILESTONES

Birthdays, anniversaries, Thanksgiving, Christmas, Mother's Day, Father's Day, Easter and Valentine's Day. These were special days for Mom and therefore us. They gave Mom an excuse to get you guys to come home. It also gave her an excuse to give you presents or something called a "sursie". I'm not sure where that word came from but I think it is synonymous with pajamas. At least for you girls.

Those milestones are probably the hardest days of the year for all of us. (The worst is probably the date she died) But we've now been through them once or twice. Each time will be and has been a little easier. I hope they don't continue to be the source of real sadness. Instead, Mom would want us to focus in on all the great memories we have of her. We have to make new ones to associate with those days so they won't be so hard. We have to go forward.

The only other option is to stay in the past and feel like nothing can ever be as good as it was. And that's just not true. Many things will never be the same but that doesn't mean that we can't have new experiences that make us just as happy. Mom was nothing if she was not positive. For her the glass was always half full. For her there was always hope and she could almost always find something good in everyone and every situation. That was what drove her and made her who she was. For this family to not go forward and make new memories would make Mom very unhappy. We will Not do that to her.

CHAPTER TWENTY

:

LIFE IS SIMPLE

For Mom, life was seemingly always busy and chaotic. Yes, she made it that way as she wasn't very good at slowing down or telling anyone "no". She liked nice things but she also liked simple things. Therefore she enjoyed cards that I would make for her even better than one purchased at the store. Even though they were corny and poorly done. I think I started writing and drawing them one year when I "mistakenly forgot" to get her something for Mother's Day. (Which actually wasn't as bad as when I remembered it and paid for "trash pickup" for a year for her. That may have been her least liked present ever. Even Megan chewed on me for that one and she was only about twelve at the time.) Anyway, she loved the cards and got to where she expected them. (with a gift or the promise of one, of course). I have added some of them on the next few pages.

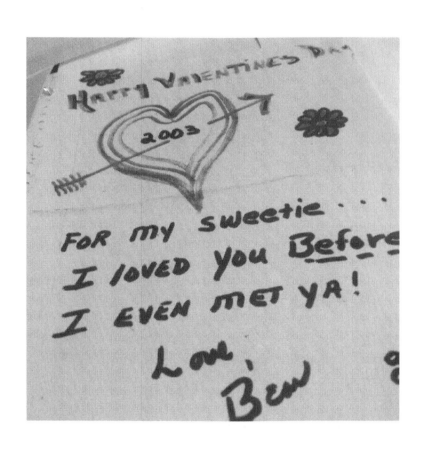

And in my heart!

Happy Birthday
Love Ya!
Bear

Cher,

I hope you know how much you mean to me. There really are no words or gifts that would fully express my faith & trust in you. You are a great Mom to the kids & many people around you.

I Love Ya,
Dean

P.S. This card gives you one free pass to Monkey around with me, anytime you want! (And a sunset in Chicago when) you & Megan go shopping, maybe some new clothes for work!

79

Happy

Anniversary!

Dec. 21
2010
(our 35th)
and last

Char,

You make me and all you touch better.
These last 4 months have been great,
just knowing that you were near. The
Lord has used you while so many around
us have been struggling. He needed you
to be available to reassure them. Yes,
you will have to go back to work
someday, but until then I'm sure
He appreciates your help, and so do I.

I love you more each day.

Ben

CHAPTER TWENTY-ONE

:

MOM'S FAMILY

Looking back, I realize that I was not "on top of my game" for a period of time after Mom died. I am sure now that I initially gave Mom's family (and some of my own too), the impression that they were not welcome at my house. That truly was not the case. I was in shock. I am not as outgoing as Mom was. As far as I was concerned there were too many people in my house asking me to make too many decisions. Decisions that I didn't want to make. I just needed to feel in control of something in my life. I felt that it was coming apart and I wanted some of it back. Deep down I knew it was never going to be the same.

I know now that I had thrown up a wall around myself and I was only letting a few people cross over it. I truly hope that Mom's family understands how hard this all was for me and forgives me for not being very open with them.

I have been around Mom's family for a very long time. I consider myself a part of that family. I hope they continue to want to be a part of our lives. They are always welcome at the farm.

This place has been a source of comfort and peace for us. I hope it continues to be for them also.

CHAPTER TWENTY-TWO

:

IT'S PERSONAL

When Mom was here, there was no subject off limits. You are quite aware of her tendency to randomly ask questions or to make statements that would catch you totally off guard. I always hated to hear the words, "we need to talk" just as I was about to fall asleep after a long day. Now, I have the opposite problem. Who do I talk things through with? Who do I tell my deepest worries and problems to? Who do I tell about my good and bad days?

Megan, you probably get to hear most of my personal fears about coping with everyday life. I am sorry but that's just the way it is. Matt, you get to hear my worries over the farming business. I guess we have always had the love of agriculture in common so it just seems fitting that we talk about those issues. We don't talk as often as Megan and I but we tend to have long conversations when we do.

I also talk to Grandpa a lot. He's my go-to guy for all things regarding religion. I have a lot of friends and they probably hear more of my worries than they really want to. My cousin and his wife catch quite a few of my questions about where I fit in the church and the community now. I also talk to aunt Nan quite often. Mostly about family. We have known each other for almost 45 years and know more about each other than we really should. ☺

That leaves my most personal issues to deal with. The things that you would normally only discuss with your spouse. These are the hardest problems to find an outlet for. I know you guys would listen but there are actually some things that you just can't tell your kids. Don't be offended! I'm sure there are plenty of things going on with you that I don't hear about. And I'm pretty sure I don't want to.

CHAPTER TWENTY-THREE

:

WORK

You know I really enjoy my jobs. Sure, there are parts of them I don't like but that is true of any job. Since closing down the tire shop, I've felt like I have had more time to devote to farming and being the township road commissioner. And of course being road commissioner with all its' prestige offsets the low pay and lousy hours and "cussings" that go with it. ☺

But, for the most part I've always felt that farming was what I was meant to do. The long hours are not just a part of it. They are essential to making it work and being successful. Since Mom died though, my perspective has changed considerably. I still love farming. Maybe now more than ever. But I feel my overall view of life has widened and I feel I have a better understanding of what's important. I now concentrate less on trying to do everything the "experts" say we should. Instead I'm trying hard to enjoy the work and the relationships with the people I do business with. Losing Mom definitely changed me. What I am really trying to do is get back the feelings I had about farming when I first started almost forty years ago.

I believe that the ag media and the ag lenders have pushed farmers to become so efficient that we can't take time to enjoy what makes this job different than most. It is a way of life. Not just a business. Since I first started farming that idea has been completely turned backwards. I understand the reasons for that push but there has to be a balance struck between working and living. Work provides routine that we need, especially after losing someone. There is a comfort in having a reason for getting up every day to go work. I am sure we all have needed that reason to put one foot in front of the other at some point in the last two years. Maybe not every day, but on those days when missing Mom is hard to get past. I am just suggesting that you don't forget to enjoy the little things along the way.

CHAPTER TWENTY-FOUR

:

MISSING MOM

I still talk to Mom a bunch. After talking to someone every day for forty years it's a hard habit to break. I still miss her. I don't know when or if that ever goes away. A lady who lost her husband over twenty years ago once said to me that, "he's only one thought away". I don't know if she originated that saying or if she heard it somewhere but it is so true. No matter what I'm doing or thinking, Mom is only one thought away. That's because my thought process is still from the perspective of Mom and I together. I may be by myself now but I haven't started thinking as a single person. I know that someday I will. Society and circumstances will push me to adapt and think only about what I want. That is something I truly worry about. That I will get used to being alone.

Being okay with living alone means that I've forgotten what it was like living with Mom. I really don't want that to happen but I know it's coming. I can feel it. It's not that I ever could forget her. Her life and mine are so mixed together that forgetting her would be impossible. It's more that I will forget what it felt like to actually be with her.

I said to Mom that if something happened to her, I would probably just sit in the recliner and watch TV. And I did. But, I've now reached the point where I can't just sit there. I get lonely for adult conversation. So I tag along sometimes with friends to their kids' events or go get groceries or to the café. I can spend a lot of time by myself but there is a limit. (I run out of things to talk to myself about) Maybe that's another reason why I'm writing this. I've already told these stories to myself and now I'm writing them down. This way when I forget some of the details about how I used to feel I can read this to remember. Don't laugh. I'm serious.

Another thing you need to know is how hard it is for me to leave home sometimes. At home I feel Mom's presence around me. This where all the good things happened. (And the hard things but even those are good memories now) It's where I feel the most secure. I was never a "world traveler" and don't think I ever will be. But some days it is especially hard to leave this house. Memories of Mom just pull me back here. Something else I am working to overcome...........

CHAPTER TWENTY-FIVE

:

SHE'S COMPLICATED

Mom was special to us. She was not perfect. Nor would she want you to think she was. (Only one man can claim that) But, I think she did have "something" that a lot of us never have. She saw life in a much wider view than I, but yet she was often confused over where she fit in this life. She was extremely confident speaking in front of a crowd but always wanted me to go first if we were in a line for something. She was complicated.

She wanted to live life to its fullest but she was as ready to meet Jesus as anyone I ever knew. She really loved her kids but they worried her more than anyone else. She could be tough. She could tell the president of a company that he was absolutely wrong about something and then ask how his family was doing. And sincerely want to know. She loved living in the country yet she never truly understood farming and how it worked. She constantly worried about money even while she was giving so much of hers away. She preached the gospel of Jesus Christ with a tattoo on her arm for all to see. She was extremely tolerant of people but you did not get between her and her children. She loved going on vacation but it was nearly impossible to get her to go on one. She liked nice things but not nearly as much as she liked babies. Of any kind or size. She often said that she loved to watch me farm but seldom wanted to be part of it. She was extremely bright about book keeping but was overdrawn in her own checking account at least ten times a year. She seemed to know so much about life but asked some of the craziest questions. She was very proficient with computers but never could run the TV remote. She traveled this country for 15 years, for work, but did not know her directions or where she was on a map. She was a great cook until she went into "experimental mode". She loved "Coach" purses and antique hat boxes equally. She hated shopping but loved to go so she could get a pedicure, drink coffee and visit. She hated a cluttered house but she was really kind of a slob. She disliked some parents but loved their children. She absolutely had no tolerance for lazy people. She both laughed and cried easily. She loved to get hugs and she loved even more to give them. She was a loyal friend. And she loved her God, her husband, her children, her family and her friends. Your Mom loved a lot. That may be the main thing that she left for us to remember about her. She loved a lot.

CHAPTER TWENTY-SIX

:

WHY MOM?

Two nights after Mom died, a group of people gathered at our church. They told stories of how Mom had touched their lives. How she had made them laugh. How she had "encouraged" them to do things for the church that they never would have done. How she made them a better person by setting an example they wanted to follow. I had never heard of people getting together for such a tribute. I would have liked to have been there and heard their kind comments but I just couldn't. It was too much for me to handle at that moment. That meeting was something very special. It proved to me that I wasn't the only one who saw what Mom had become.

I still miss her greatly. Maybe now more than ever. I'm just able to handle that emotion better after a year and a half. Do I understand why God took her so early? No. But, I do believe he had a reason. A purpose in His master plan. There is a line in a country song that says, "funny when you're dead, how people start listening".(If I Die Young by The Band Perry) Grandpa said that the only reason that he could come up with, for God to take her when she was doing so much for Him, was that her death would bring even more people to believe in Jesus. And that she had already reached as many people as would listen while she was alive. I think Grandpa is right. Mom's early death shocked a lot of folks into getting their own lives prepared.

I once said to you that Mom showed us how to live but not how to live without her. I was wrong. Her example of what real faith in God looks like was what she was supposed to be showing us. Don't ever doubt that Mom is okay where she is now. Wherever Heaven is. She knew where she was going and was excited about going there. And I believe Mom is at peace for the first time in her life. She was complicated but on this subject she was clear. You believe in God and his Son and you will find peace. Just that simple.

CHAPTER TWENTY-SEVEN

:

MOVING FORWARD

This past weekend (June 3, 2012) our family and our church family gathered to watch Grayson Keith Free be baptized. It was bittersweet for all of us. Feelings of great pride and wonder were coupled with wishing Mom was there to see it. Well, I believe she was! Did you notice where the scripture for the sermon came from? It was from John 3: 2-17. It included the verse that Mom had tattooed on her wrist from John 3:16. The pastor did not plan that. He hadn't even thought about the significance of using that verse until some of us mentioned it to him. Yes, Mom was there. Pushing us all to move forward and to remind us that she's still here. In many ways. She wants us to live life again and believe. And she wants to see us when we are done here. She is waiting. (Probably not very patiently) It is up to us to do what is necessary to get there.

As her husband I worry that people will forget her. Maybe that's another reason to write this. There will always be a "history" of Mom, especially for the grandkids that didn't get to meet her.

Even as we attempt to carry on without her. She cannot be replaced and we will never forget.

Is that the bottom line? Is that the real reason I had to tell these stories? I've struggled with the reason since I began thinking about writing them. I actually stopped writing six months ago because I couldn't come up with a reason to continue.

Recently, I woke up from a sound sleep at 3 o'clock in the morning. I had something on my mind but I was having trouble grasping it. Then it became clear. The ultimate reason why I had to write this story. This is my witness to God and Mom that I have enough faith to go on. That this family will continue what she and I started 40 years ago. What began as hope and a dream of two young kids will not end with her passing. It's what families do. They look to the future at something that is bigger than all of us. It's the reason God puts us here. We believe, like Mom, in Something that cannot be touched and Someone who cannot be seen. Faith. It is the reason. Pretty simple.

I Loved Ya before I even met Ya,

Dad

TWO OF THE PICTURES TAKEN ON GRAYSON'S BIG DAY ARE ON THE FOLLOWING PAGES

GETTING BAPTIZED !

THE FREE FAMILY MOVES FORWARD

Grayson Keith Free
Born--December 02, 2011

Dedicated to God– June 3, 2012

CHAPTER TWENTY-EIGHT

:

THE WRITING OF THIS BOOK

This part of the book was actually written over a six week period starting May 1st, 2012. (Yes, right in the middle of planting season) Sometimes it was easy to come up with the words. Sometimes I struggled as I relived the details of what I was writing. Sometimes my hand was steady (it was originally written by hand, in cursive). Sometimes I was shaking. Sometimes I laughed as I wrote. Many times I cried and had to stop for a while. Sometimes a thought or a story would come to me late at night or very early in the morning. I just put down what came to me with whatever emotion that brought it out. It has been very helpful to write these letters even though it has been equally as hard. It includes my personal feelings. Not everyone will agree with them. Because of my time constraints, sometimes it reads sort of disjointed. Like me. Like my life is now. But this is what it is, seven pens and 250 sheets of paper later.

Dad

PART TWO

of

LETTERS FROM HOME

"WHERE DO I GO FROM HERE?"

Written from July 2012 to June 2013

One and a half to two and a half years

after Mom passed

CHAPTER ONE

:

WHERE AM I NOW?

I said in the first part of this book that I was afraid that I would get used to being alone. I'm not sure I even knew why at the time, but I think I do now. After coming home to a big empty house for another year with no one to talk to, I am starting to realize what being alone really is. Yes, I know I can talk to you guys and others by e-mail, texting and the phone anytime. But that's not the same as having another person here with me. I now know what the change from being married and part of a team really means. This is a couple's world and I am no longer a part of it.

I don't want you to worry that I can't handle living alone. That's just not true. It's just that I don't want to forget what it's like to have someone special in your life. I am doing well. Great actually. Considering how low I was when I started this journey. But I know there's more because I had it once.

I operate now almost methodically and without passion. That's the thing that is missing. If this goes on too long, I worry that I'll become so used to being independent that I won't care to make any change. Don't you think that Mom will be very disappointed in me if I don't retain at least "some of what she taught me?" ☺

One thing that I have learned is that every few months a new chapter begins in my life. This journey of grief and learning, or re-learning who we are, continually changes our perspective. I suppose that was true before, but I just wasn't paying attention. Now that I've learned how to survive on my own, I think I'm ready for the next step.

I've found myself wondering if I want to go through the rest of my life alone. Or do I want to open the door and let someone else in? This may be the scariest part of my journey. There will be new obstacles that I am sure I haven't anticipated.

After I first lost Mom, we had such an enormous amount of support, both physically and spiritually. Someone was at the house all the time. That is exactly what I needed then. But after a couple of months I was ready for peace and quiet to return to my home. I needed time to think and time to process what had actually happened.

I truly needed to be alone and wanted to be able to choose when I did not want to be. I realized that I really needed to figure out who I was without Mom. But, as time has passed that has changed. I now want to spend less time alone. I need more time with people. I now feel the need for more. Period. I am not satisfied with what I have. I think I would like a companion. If it doesn't happen. I will go on. It's just not going to be as fulfilling to go it alone as it could be with someone.

My brother Stan was about 13 years old when he smashed his finger. I'm sure it hurt like heck. His response was something I'll never forget. He said," too old to cry, too young to cuss!" I feel his dilemma. I sometimes feel too old to start dating and too young to spend the rest of my life alone.

I know that you shouldn't have to change who you are to be with someone. It should feel natural and easy to be together. But, it's so scary for me to even think about! I wouldn't be in control................

CHAPTER TWO

:

WHO IS IN CHARGE?

Before Mom died I always thought that I knew what I needed and wanted out of my life. I felt like I had some control over how things turned out. But after Mom died I was lost for a long time and probably in shock. I soon learned that I couldn't control what had happened, what was happening and very little of what was going to happen in the future.

Maybe that was the point that God was trying to make with me. In a very tough way. By taking the person I loved more than anything or anyone. Maybe I had gotten too cocky. I actually thought I was in control. How wrong I was! No matter how hard I worked or looked into the future, I never would have predicted the changes in my life that began the day Mom died. Looking back now, I realize how foolish I was to think that I was in full control of everything that happened.

I now believe that God has a plan for us even before we are conceived. We can make good choices and our journey here on earth will be less painful. But, in the end if we follow God's plan and let Him lead, this journey will be so much easier. He is in control! We are here a very short time and will hopefully make the best of it. But the last I checked there was only one person to walk this earth that was perfect. I'm really certain that it's not me.

So, I have had to learn to accept help from God, my family and my friends. I have had to learn that I cannot do this life alone. This hasn't been easy and I struggle with it every day. (I am a man after all! And worse yet, an independent farmer! We don't need help!) But the fact is, losing Mom is hard! It's the hardest thing I have ever done. I truly have needed a lot of help to keep me moving forward.

In the last two years I have been worried about a whole bunch of things. Losing Mom, figuring out where I belong, closing the tire business, resigning as road commissioner and allowing people to read my inner most thoughts are a few.

But, it has made me focus on what is important. I am sure that I have done things that I have never thought I would. I have had to learn that I am not always in charge of my life. I have had to let others help me.

Life is short. We've certainly had to learn that. One year ago I wasn't ready to even think about being with someone other than Mom. Now, I am at least ready to talk about the possibility. Relax guys. I am fine and no, Mom cannot be replaced. (nor could I replace anyone else) But I truly believe that I haven't really moved on with my life, or can I suggest that you do, if I won't seriously entertain the idea of finding a new companion.

Whenever I get the feeling that things aren't going the way I want them to, God reminds me that my plan is flawed. Because it's my plan. It's not always about me.

I was sitting at my desk recently, paying bills and thinking about how I was going to deal with a particular situation that had been bugging me all week. In the background I had Mom's I-pod playing quietly and wasn't really paying any attention to the music. Mom had downloaded the songs over her last two to three years and it was randomly playing them. Don't ask me why it was randomly picking out songs to play. As you know, Bob only taught me how to turn it on a short time ago.

While contemplating my problem, and how I could control the outcome, I realized the music had stopped and someone was speaking instead. I reached over and turned up the volume and found out it was Steven Curtis Chapman's wife, Mary Beth. (He is a well-known gospel singer and inspirational speaker) Anyway, Mary Beth was telling stories about their lives and how their faith had been recently deeply tested. They had lost one of their little girls when she had run in front of a car. According to her, the accident had truly devastated their family. But with a tremendous amount of support from friends and family and of course, their faith in God, they are moving forward.

I quickly rewound to the beginning of her speech. (Yes, I know that Bob is surprised I could do that.) She began by listing three things she had told God she would never do. She said she would never adopt children, never home school her kids, and never speak in public. Of course, they now have three adopted kids, she's home schooling them and obviously she has begun telling people about their journey of grief after losing their daughter. She also said that her husband and her had a rigid plan for their lives that they had mapped out when they got married. She was going to work to support them while he finished college and starting a family would come much later.

Their plan really didn't work out like they thought it would. A year and a half into their marriage, they had a new baby and their apartment had burned to the ground after she left a baby bottle heating on the stove. It was then that they first realized that God had their story already written and it wasn't exactly like theirs. And they needed to stop trying to control every aspect of their lives and follow His plan. He was in charge.

Following God's plan is hard. We humans, by nature, think that our plan is better. We think that we can get back to God's plan as soon as we've taken care of ours first. That usually doesn't work out. God doesn't make mistakes. We do. And He has an endless number of ways to get His point across. ☺

Very soon after Mom died, I realized that I wasn't up to the task of controlling my life. It truly brought home the point that I needed to trust that God's plan was better than mine. I really believe that if I'm meant to find a new companion that it will happen regardless of how many mistakes I make along the way.

I once said to a friend of mine that I refused to go looking for someone new in the bars. Therefore, I probably would have a hard time finding someone out here in the cornfields of Illinois. He reminded me that if God wanted two people to get together that He could make that happen. I think I'll go with that. If it doesn't happen then it must not have been part of my story. But, if it does happen there is something important that you guys need to remember. You didn't "choose" your mother. I did. So you'll have to trust that I get it right again or I won't choose at all.

CHAPTER THREE

:

A NEW BEGINNING

And so begins a new chapter. The one that starts the process of actually looking forward. I told you before that I couldn't really look much past next week. I am tired of living that way. I think I am ready to think longer term. That's something I haven't done since Mom passed.

In writing this part I am reminded of a statement that Matt Damon(playing the part of Benjamin Mee) makes in the movie, "We Bought a Zoo". In it he says that life is a series of adventures in which we must find, "20 seconds of insane courage and embarrassing bravery", or we will miss opportunities that we'll regret our whole lives. This is one of those times in my life. I will need those 20 seconds. Many times. I hope I am up to the task.

Whoever, if ever, I find someone to finish this life with, they will not be a clone of Mom. You may even be surprised at who I am attracted to. But she will have to have some of the same traits. They may just be in a completely different package. She will have to be a hard worker, not lazy. She will have to be passionate about her family and friends and have a good sense of humor. And above all, she will have to believe in Jesus Christ. She will absolutely have to "get it". By that I mean she will have to understand what's important in life. She won't necessarily have to be as vocal about her faith as Mom, but she must believe.

So the next step is to make the determination as to whether I am willing to play it safe for the rest of my life. Or am I willing to make the effort and risk the fact that I may be rejected. Even worse would be to find someone I truly cared for, and then lose her too. The fact is that you "can't have your cake and eat it too". I know that if you find love again, the chances are 50/50 that you risk burying someone again. Kind of a catch-22. Risk and reward. Love and another broken heart. Not an easy step to take.

CHAPTER FOUR

:

DON'T LOOK BACK

Someone who had lost their husband once told me, "Don't make any big decisions for at least two years". She felt that you are not really capable until you've gone through at least that much of the grieving process. Even things that you are struggling with, such as a job that's not going well, are important to keep doing. She said, "They are at least a familiar reference point in your life that haven't changed. There are enough changes in your life. You shouldn't add to them right now".

I do agree that someone who loses their spouse should not make any "life changing" decisions for a while. That is actually true for losing anyone that you were that connected to. Although I don't think that two years is the "industry wide" standard that we all should follow. We all handle grief differently and at our own pace. I believe that most of us will know when the time is right to make those important decisions. I also believe that most of us would benefit from seeking out someone to talk to about our loss. And I also believe that we should not judge people on their decisions. We will make some good ones and some bad ones. It's just part of the process.

I told you earlier that I spent most of my life as part of a team with Mom. Therefore, it has taken me a while to learn who I am as a single person. It is an ongoing process. I am still learning what my individual likes and dislikes are. I have been forced into making some major decisions in the last 2 years and at this time don't regret any of them. I wish I had been given two years before I had to make them. But life rolls on whether you get on the train or not.

I know you guys have also had to make some very big changes in your lives since Mom died. I hope you don't look back and wish you had made different ones. Winston Churchill once said, "The heaviest burden to carry is something you did yesterday". Even if everything hasn't worked out as you had planned, those decisions are part of your journey here on earth. I'm suggesting that you, (and I) just learn from them and move on.

CHAPTER FIVE

:

CONFIDENCE AND GUILT

When you're young and in love you really don't think about the practical problems that can and will come up in a marriage. As they say, ignorance is bliss. This is a good thing, in many ways. Otherwise, very few people would ever get married or have children. ☺ But, at my age and with a lot of experience and time to think, I can come up with a lot of reasons to never marry again. I'm pretty sure that many widowers feel the same way.

We'll get into the other reasons soon but first we need to discuss what I think is the number one reason that most of us do not think we'll ever find someone new. The reason is confidence. I have told you before how losing Mom really took away my social confidence. It shook me to the core. (Once again, I know not everyone responds the same way)

I've finally got back close to where I was before but now I am thinking about doing something that may set me right back in that hole. Starting a new relationship would be taking a huge scary step forward!

Really, who would want an old gray haired, out of shape farmer who lives in the middle of a cornfield? And has the emotional baggage of losing the only person he ever loved? I wonder if, only another person with the same experience can understand me at all. I could be wrong though. There are probably people of great compassion that might get it. I just know that before it happened to me, I did not.

And if I found someone who has been through this, wouldn't they be carrying a lot of baggage as well? Is that a recipe for disaster or am I so lacking in confidence that I'm just borrowing trouble?

At this age, you are what you are. It's too late for me or anyone else to change. We are a byproduct of our life experiences and our environment. And if you need to change to be with someone it probably won't work anyway. So, lack of confidence. Shaken to the core. I believe that is the top reason for us widowers to not ever marry again. At least it is for me at this point in my life and as I talk with many others I can tell they have the same problem. Regardless of what they say or how they act.

Do I spend the rest of my life actually living or do I just coast to the finish line by myself? Is it already too late? Am I already used to being alone? And can I make the changes needed to adapt to someone new? Answers to come in the future.

I believe guilt is probably a very close second to lack of confidence. For me to have feelings for another woman, I have to get past that. I know that Mom would not want me to sit here by myself every night if I have the opportunity to spend time with another woman. I know, in my mind, this is absolutely true. But, in my weaker moments my heart is not so sure. Being as connected to Mom as I am, will always remain. As a widower we don't just feel guilty about being with someone new, we feel guilty about still being here period. Survivors' guilt I suppose. We also feel guilty if we find ourselves too happy or having too much fun.

But then again, I must have made some progress or I wouldn't be thinking about these things at all……………

CHAPTER SIX

:

ACCEPTANCE

It would be really important to me, if I found someone new, that you guys would accept that person. It would be even more important that you trust me to find the right person. Ninety nine percent of the time I am here by myself so this decision affects me much more than you.

It is also important to me that my other family members and friends accept my decision. Many have told me that they would not want to go home to an empty house every night and that they understand how lonely my life must be. I really appreciate them saying that but wonder just how they would react if I brought someone new to this community.

I probably worry even more about taking someone new to church. Will people there accept her when Mom and I were so active there together?

I have to keep reminding myself that if I do find someone, it will not be the same relationship I had with Mom. Everything in my life has changed. And I have changed. I cannot duplicate exactly what we had. But, I want something similar. This is a couple's world. I've always enjoyed that feeling and I would like to try that again. I miss that interaction and intimacy. If I get the chance, I hope I'll "dance".

I also worry that you guys will think that I won't be there for you. That someone else will take your place. You need to know that, just like Mom, you can't be replaced. I will always only have one daughter, one son, one daughter-in-law and one son-in-law. That also doesn't mean that I don't have room in my heart to love other people, but it will never be the same as the love I have for you. It will just be different.

CHAPTER SEVEN

:

HERE WE GO?

I believe that you would rather I not find someone new. Actually, it would be easier for all of us to just leave things as they are now. I know it's easier to deal with just me, than to accommodate someone who is different from Mom. (I think I'm pretty stable, sane and don't ask for too much) ☺ But my life would not be as full as it could be.

Please look at it from my view. You have someone to go home to every night. And even though you lost Mom, you still have your best friend. Mom was my best friend. She was the only person I ever dated or loved. If she had lived to be 100, I would have been right there with her. But, she didn't and now we all must move forward and try to live without her. I will never forget her or stop loving her. But, I am ready to see what's next in my life.

About three months after Mom died, Megan and I went to town to get me some groceries. On the way she asked me if I thought I would ever be happy again. I said, "I sure hope so because I would hate to feel like this for the rest of my life".

I think I am ready to start the next leg in that journey. I think I am ready to stop feeling "like this". I will need your help. I will need your approval and acceptance. I've already asked Mom. She's okay with it. I hope you are too. It's time for us all to be happy again.

LOVE YA,
DAD

CHAPTER EIGHT

:

AFTERTHOUGHTS

I don't know why but for some reason when spring comes, I start writing. I guess, like winter I have an accumulation of thoughts that I need to wipe clean and start anew. I enjoy writing. I recommend it. You don't have to be a Pulitzer Prize winning author to find comfort in it. For me, it's very therapeutic. It helps me to look back on the past year and organize the significant events that have taken place. It helps me to see which way I am headed.

The thoughts in this part of the book began coming to me soon after I had finished the first part. I finally started writing them down on whatever pieces of paper I could find nearby. After about four months, I once again realized that I had quite a pile of notes. So, I decided to start writing again. Unlike the first part where there seemed to be a definitive progression of events to write about, these thoughts seemed to come from all directions. It took me a while to realize that they were mostly about preparing you (and me) in the event that I might try seeing someone.

Deep thoughts about my future. Something my friend, Bill Campbell taught me were worth more than material things. (At least that's why he said he wasn't getting anyone presents for Christmas one year. He said he was just sending all of his friends "deep thoughts" instead.) ☺

Anyway, good luck in figuring out where I was going with this part. I'm not sure that I even know. And do keep in mind that I am not desperate or so lonely that I can't go on. My life is better than most and as our pastor says, "Better than I deserve". Many issues I had one year ago have improved. I'm no longer as worried about many of the things I wrote about in the first part of this book.

But, it's funny and ironic that I set out to convince you (and me) that I was ready to take the next step in moving on. Instead, after writing my thoughts out to make them more clear, I may have scared myself into doing nothing. I may just decide it's too late in my life to start over. I can do that. I'm in charge. Right???????

We'll talk next spring,

DAD

PART THREE

of

LETTERS FROM HOME

"RANDOM THOUGHTS"

:

Written from June 2013 to June 2014

Two and a half to three and a half years

after Mom passed

CHAPTER ONE

:

RESTLESS

Since Mom passed, there seems to be so many "mysteries" that I must solve. But slowly I am unraveling some of them. For example, I am one of the most dependable people you know. If I say that I will do something, I do it. That's not bragging. It's just a description of what I am like. If I say that I will meet you somewhere, then I will be there. Probably 15 minutes early.

But, lately I have had to veer off my normal routine. I get restless. I have to do the unexpected and unpredictable. For a long time, I couldn't figure out what was wrong with me. Now, I think I know.

Every once in a while, I find myself out doing something with you or other family or friends, and not able to focus on what we are doing. Something is missing. Or someone is missing. I'm out enjoying myself but it doesn't feel right.

It finally struck me that Mom isn't with us. That's the problem. I know she's gone and never coming back. But I can't get over the feeling that I should be at home waiting for her to return from wherever she is. I feel like I'm in the wrong place with the wrong people. Even though I'm with the people that love me. THAT'S what restless feels like.

I know it doesn't make sense. It's not practical or probably even rational. But, sometimes that's how I feel. It's no ones' fault. It's not even guilt. (That's a whole different feeling) It's just an unexplainable feeling of a habit that's so hard to break.

So, when I feel this way I have to do something different. I have to change what I have always done and refocus on something new. That's when I show up at your house unannounced, give you a call, or take off on an "adventure". I'm not the only one that feels this way. I've seen it in some of my widow friend's faces. I know what they are feeling. I just thought I should at least try to explain it to you.

CHAPTER TWO

:

DECISIONS

I've always been decisive and more than willing to make the needed decisions about our family and our business. I always felt that I knew where we were headed. (Of course I "let" Mom make a few decisions too) ☺

For the first six months after Mom died though, it seemed like there was always someone pushing me to make a decision about something or someone. And now I have to rely on family and friends to discuss things, when all I really want is to talk to Mom. This is so different than when you make "team" decisions like I talked about in an earlier chapter. And it puts so much pressure on you at a time when you truly don't want any pressure at all. It wears you down, and at least in my case, made me very indecisive about what were routine decisions. I thought this indecisiveness all started in the hall of the hospital where the doctor asked me what funeral home he should call, and continued with medical, financial, family and business decisions needing to be made. But looking back, I now believe this feeling of not wanting to make a decision was triggered before that. I now believe it started right after I told the doctor to stop working on Mom and "let her go". That's the decision I had to make without anyone's help. A decision I wanted to make so no one else had to live with it. A decision I knew she would want me to make. And a decision I made with confidence that day.

There's just some days, though, that my heart doesn't seem to be in agreement with my brain.

CHAPTER THREE

:

CONFUSED

It's no wonder I'm sometimes confused and torn as to how to live. On one hand I want to slow down time. The farther I move away from the day Mom died, I know I will forget even more things I once knew about her and the life we had together. My heart says that I don't want that but it is inevitable, so I feel guilty. I wonder, not only where time has gone since she passed, but where time has gone in general.

On the other hand, I want to speed time up. The further I get away from losing Mom, the more it seems okay that I am moving forward. I can look back and say that it's been two or three years since she has passed so it's okay if I think about moving my personal life along.

In the end, time moves on. And the world moves on. And our family moves forward and changes regardless of how I feel or what I do.

I guess I'll just have to take the journey and see where it leads me.

CHAPTER FOUR

:

GAVIN'S DAY

I was talking to aunt Nan on the phone a few days before Gavin's baptism and she mentioned that she had purchased a gift for him. I asked her for what occasion. Seriously. She said it was a baptism gift, of course. Now, you would think that after two and a half years after Mom's passing, that I would be in the habit of knowing that it was up to me to get a gift for such major occasions. I had thought to get a few extra groceries and had remembered to make sure that the sheets on your beds were clean. But, it had never occurred to me that I should get Gavin a gift, and a card for the proud parents.

This occasion just reinforced my inability to go from working my way through life with someone, to going it alone. When someone in the community passes it is now my sole responsibility to send them a card or stop by and see them. If someone close to me has a birthday or anniversary (or even a baptism), it is my responsibility to send a card or a gift. And if there is a function at the church that requires a donation of time or money, I need to get that done.

When one of you needs to talk about your jobs, or life's surprises in general, it is now my responsibility to be there for you. Even if I don't always have a good answer.

(Writing this actually reminded me of the time I took Megan shopping for a new bra. Yep, that's not a misprint. And probably the last time Mom entrusted me with this much responsibility. Megan was going to some dress up affair, like a prom or a homecoming dance and Mom was unexpectedly called out of town on business on the day they were to purchase one. She insisted that I was quite capable of handling the problem, no matter how loudly I protested. You must remember, of course, that I grew up with three brothers and had about as much experience in this department as she had digging post holes.

So, off we went to the mall. Me doing my fatherly duties and all. Looking for a strapless bra for a formal gown. That was the extent of her advice. Mom may have thought she won this battle but it cost her dearly. As I remember the process, I walked Megan to the desk in the women's clothing department of the local Bergner's store. And there I did what most fathers would do. I told the clerk that my daughter needed some kind of a bra "thing". And that I would be over looking at tools at Sears (like a macho-man should). And that Megan should come get me when she was ready to pay. The clerk asked how much I was willing to spend. I answered with all the dignity of a farmer in the bra section of a women's clothing store could and said, "Don't really have any limit". (I just needed one fast so we could get out of there before anyone I knew recognized me).

That, of course was the exact wrong thing to say to a woman who probably had several female children of her own at home. (I should have noticed sooner, that locket hanging around her neck with a picture of three girls in it). I am certain she was smirking all the way to the back of the store where the diamond encrusted bras are stored under lock and key. There, my wonderful daughter, with the smirking store clerk guiding her, picked out a bra that only movie stars and reality TV personalities can afford. I think we had to stop at the bank on the way home and mortgage the truck to cover it.)

Anyway, I must admit that Mom usually took care of sending cards and getting appropriate presents for most functions. But now it's just me. I am it. And I not only have the responsibilities that I used to have but I have hers also. She was always busy. And I now know why. Sometimes I do okay. Sometimes I feel like I am on top of things. And sometimes I feel so inadequate for the task.

You should know one thing though. When it comes to all four of you, I will never stop trying to be there in any way I can. Always.

Even if it costs me another year of truck payments.

CHAPTER FIVE

:

SHE'S STILL HERE

In the movie "One Day", a man and a woman finally get married after 20 years of never being on quite the same page in their lives. They had always been great friends but somehow it took them that long to get the timing right.

Shortly after getting married, the woman is run over by a truck while riding a bicycle. The man is overcome with grief, as you can imagine. The night of the funeral he goes on an all- night bender. A friend finds him beaten and passed out, and calls his father. The man's father asked his friend to bring him to his house. (His mother had passed away 10 years earlier from cancer).

When the guy finally wakes up the next day, his father offers him one simple suggestion. He said, "I think you should stop acting like this and start living like your wife is still here".

That was it. That was all he had to say. In other words, he was telling him that she made him a better person when she was alive, so it stands to reason that if he conducted his life as if she's still here, then he would   have to live up to that expectation and actually be a better person.

Made me think of your Mom..........

CHAPTER SIX

:

LOST OPPORTUNITIES

All of you came home yesterday. We were celebrating Grandma's 80th birthday. We had a great time. But we also accomplished another milestone while you were here. We (including the busy grandkids) gathered in my bedroom and sorted through Mom's clothes. Megan, you had the wonderful idea of donating them to a women's organization in Peoria. They help women go back into the workplace after getting out of an abusive relationship. Mom was very successful in her career and would be so happy that they went to improving the lives and self-esteem of other working moms.

I found the process quite bittersweet. Another small piece of who Mom was, has left me. We laughed at some of her clothing choices. Some just jumped out at you and said, "Mom". They were a part of what we remember and cherish about her unique style. It was sad to see them go. But, I knew it was time. It was time to take another step forward and remember what is important.

We all know that "you can't take it with you". Your car, your house, your land, or your money. And you only take one set of clothes.

The process prompted me to ask the question, "Can you really take anything of value with you when you go"? I could only come up with one answer. Lost opportunities.

When you die you take with you every chance you ever had or ever will have to effect the lives of those around you, in a good way. At least after you die, you will never know if you did. You really only get a short period of time to make an impact. The time goes by so fast. Sometimes a lot faster than we could ever anticipate. Like losing Mom in one day.

So we can do like she showed us. We can follow her example and live like today might be our last. It just may be. And we don't want to miss our only opportunities to do the right thing. To be the person God wants us to be.

Mom was so much more than the clothes she wore. She left us with so many memories that are special for each of us. And she left us with the knowledge that she would want us to move forward with our lives and be happy. The clothes are gone.

But her memory never will be.

CHAPTER SEVEN

:

A CHRISTMAS STORY

Shortly after Mom and I got married I started sending out an annual Christmas poem that I wrote. They were quite silly but did manage to update our friends on the previous year and what occurred with our family. Sometime in the 90's I stopped. I guess I just didn't feel like writing them anymore. Since then several friends and family have tried to get me to start writing them again. I still wasn't interested.

This year, in late November I sent out an e-mail to you. In it I joked that the items on the included list were the only Christmas presents acceptable for your Dad. You always start requesting ideas for me for Christmas about Thanksgiving, so I decided to go with a kind of pre-emptive strike with some silly stuff.

Megan fired off a scathing e-mail response. In it she included the only three things that were acceptable for me to get her for Christmas. They included a large cash infusion, a snow blower and a new Christmas card poem. She didn't get the cash but Bob and she did get the snow blower and the poem on the following pages.

A CHRISTMAS STORY FOR MEGAN

Merry Christmas!
Be of good cheer!
You need not be worried,
The King is still here!

The year of 2012,
Ended on a sad note.
We lost another loved one, (whose toughness)
Was the story he wrote.

This year we asked God,
To help us to heal.
Could we please make it through?
A year without losing?
So all could re-coop,
In a way of their choosing.

God blessed those around,
Our bright Christmas tree.
And gave us a child,
Gavin. Knox. Free.

He came to life,

The same date as his Daddy.
And I hope he's as ornery,
May you have patience, Matty.
Yes, Matt is all over,
This country of ours.
His job keeps him busy
And out of the bars!

Candace is often, alone with the boys,
To cook, to clean, to pick up the toys.
She often is tired,
She's often worn out,
But the boys make her smile,
As they scamper about!

Bob and Megan are nearby,
And do lots of sittin too.
I'm so proud of the wonderful,
Job that they do.

They walk and they rock,
To keep the boys quiet.
If I could keep up, I
Wouldn't need my fried chicken diet!

Gray yells out their names,
As they walk through the door.
Uncle Bob grabs a ball,
And goes up for the score!

Gavin is crawling,
And jabbering too.
Meg says he's a sweetheart,
He'll cuddle with you!

I won re-election,
But soon turned it down.
The voters were disappointed,
And gave many a frown.

Danny called me a quitter,
I can't disagree.
But they will get by,
Without the likes of me.

My biggest worry, now that I've resigned,
Is not what everyone thinks,
Not Danny, not Russ, not even Bob,
It's what Molly will say,
About me, not having a job!

Last spring started off,
With raining and thunder.
It flooded the ground.
My bottoms went under!

The water shut off,
The 4th of July.
It seemed no more drops,
Could fall from the sky!

I worried and fretted,
I watched and I waited.
I couldn't believe,
The rain had abated! (BIG word)

But somehow the crops,
Were still very good.
We'll be able to farm,
One more year in the "hood".

We were all so excited,
We jumped in the air!
Until someone uttered,
The words, Obamacare.

Now we're once again depressed,
A smile we cannot muster.
Who would have thought?
They could produce such a cluster!

But be not dismayed,
Do not have any doubt,
Christmas is coming,
It's what the season's about.

God sent His Son,
To show us the way.
Heaven is the goal,
To get there one day.

We miss those who went before us,
We don't know all the answers.
But it makes for good "questions",
To start out the year.
We will always remember,
Who's Not present here.

Many blessings have,
Been given this year,
So get into the spirit,
Pass on some Christmas cheer!

When life gets you down,
Remember to dream,
Just think of Mom's favorite words,
From JOHN 3, VERSE 16 !

MERRY CHRISTMAS! 2013

DAD

CHAPTER EIGHT

:

IT'S SPRING AND LIFE IS SIMPLE

It's spring! At least according to the calendar. And here I am writing again. Am I where I thought I would be when I wrote last spring? No. Did I have impossible expectations one year ago? Probably.

I told you last spring that I was ready to at least consider looking at the possibility of spending time with someone. Well, I have considered the possibilities and obviously not acted on any of them. I may never.

One year ago I was just getting used to the idea of being proactive in my search for a companion. Over the last year I have let my mind wonder about what it could be like to start a new relationship. I was worried last year that it might already be too late for me to change. And right this very moment, I would say that's a very real possibility.

My life is pretty simple. More so than it ever has been. I can pick up and go whenever I want. I know there is always plenty of alone time to finish what I need to do later. I see how overwhelmed some of my friends are in their daily lives. And I realize that other than the fact that I am alone, my life is pretty satisfying.

This question keeps coming up though. Do I want to change my life and get in a much more complicated version of living? There are sacrifices to be made in a serious relationship at any age. But, when you are young you don't realize what they are and how many. You really don't care because it is new and wonderful.

But, I am no longer young. I am not so blind and can anticipate the problems of blending two families this late in the game. And I obviously question why anyone would want to hang out with a worn out old farmer. I'm not completely ruling it out. I'm just not as optimistic as I was, even one year ago.

CHAPTER NINE

:

WHEREVER YOU ARE

In conversations with you lately, I realized that I had not done a very good job of explaining how Mom and I came to the decision of raising our family in a cornfield. You see, we could have chosen to move to town where there were more opportunities for all of us. But we decided this where we wanted to be. I could have stayed in college and gone on to some other career but we consciously made the decision to move to the country and raise our children in a very traditional way. It didn't just happen. I wanted to farm. We made that choice. Just like every other farmer does. It's in our blood. And we hoped that by doing so we would be giving you a wonderful foundation based on family and religious values. The "home place" has been a central part of our family for over 150 years. Yes, I also know that all things come to an end and so will this. But, until then it will always be a place many people, including you, call home. A place where you can relax and escape from the tremendous pressures the world puts on people today, especially children. We always expect you to act in a respectful manner when you are here. But we also try to not judge your decisions or actions to make the right choices.

So, I want you to be clear. We actually made the choice to make this the best life we could here by becoming involved in our church, our school and our community. That led us to be on committees and boards and take an active interest in the activities that you wanted to do. It caused us to sink some roots here and to make some commitments. We were determined to not let our decision to hold you back in any way. And it did not. It truly added to your opportunities.

My point is that you can do the same! Wherever you are, you should make that where you are happiest. Get involved and make where you live where you want to be. God put you there for a reason. Find out what that reason is. In other words, be content with where you are and with what you have. Someone will always have more stuff than you. But no amount of money can buy more happiness than you can already afford.

CHAPTER TEN

:

YOU JUST NEVER KNOW

I recently saw the movie, "Heaven is for Real". I had already read the book so I had a pretty good idea what it was all about. But, what I wasn't ready for was how it affected me. As soon as I got home I had to pick up pen and paper and tell you a story about something that happened recently.

About a month ago I was talking to a friend on my cell phone as I was driving a tractor to the far end of my farm. We were discussing my seed corn order. At the end of the conversation he told me that some mutual friend's daughter had miscarried her baby that morning.

I punched off the phone and stopped the tractor. I felt I should do something or say something for that couple as they have been great friends to me and you since losing Mom. I just wasn't sure what I had to offer them in the way of comfort. Eventually, I typed up the following text. "Just heard about your loss. So very sorry. God and Cheryl are going to be busy. But they can handle it. Thinking of you. Barry"

Five short sentences. I was about to hit send when I began to doubt what I had done. I wondered if it was appropriate. I wondered if they felt the same way as me. That Mom is in Heaven and one of her many duties (because one obviously wouldn't be enough) is surely to take care of the babies that our family and our church family has lost. I struggled with what to do. Would my words offend them? Or were they the right words at the right time? I had many doubts but someone kept telling me to push the button. So I did.

Very quickly both of my friends responded with something like, "Thanks for thinking of us". They didn't appear to be upset so I continued on with my work and didn't really think about it anymore.

But, last Saturday changed all of that. I was at a funeral and was waiting in the church basement while the family went to the cemetery. I was visiting with a friend when I received a text from someone that there was a water problem at one of the farms I rented. He wanted me to call him so I headed across the room to go outside and make the call. About halfway there, the lady who I had texted the five sentences to, met me in the middle of the room. She said that she had been wanting to call me but decided against it because not only did she have something to tell me but she also wanted to give me a hug.

She went on to say that she hoped I wouldn't be upset with her but she just had to tell her daughter about the text I had sent after she lost the baby. Her daughter's response truly was unexpected. She said, "Oh, Mom, that was one of the first things I thought of. That my baby will be okay until I get there because Cheryl is there to take of it". I was caught completely off guard and somewhat embarrassed. I managed to say something like,

"I'm glad you liked it" as she gave me a big hug. I then went outside to make my phone call.

I am telling you this story to make two points. First, is that what I said in that text ended up helping me as much as it helped her. It was quite comforting to know that someone else also believes, that Mom never got to experience being a Grandma here on earth, because God had other plans for her in Heaven.

My second point is this. You should never be embarrassed to tell someone something that comes from your heart. We should not question our ability to positively affect someone with just a few simple words. Five short sentences. How many times do we almost offer our support but hold back for fear of it being taken the wrong way?

There is a small part of the "Heaven is for Real" movie that deals with the little boy meeting his unborn sister in Heaven. I certainly did not expect that to be the part that touched me the most.

A text or an email or even a phone call. You never know when something so small, might help someone when they are struggling. We need to be confident that when God wants to use us to help someone, He will also give you the right words. We only have to accept them and have a little faith.

Because you just never know.

CHAPTER ELEVEN

:

HELP ME OUT!

Am I really living? To me, living includes loving someone special and experiencing all of the emotions that go with that. When I lost Mom, the only emotions that I could feel were anger, guilt, grief and anxiety. Those feelings were so raw and powerful that they overrode anything else that I might have wanted to feel.

But, eventually, I learned to accommodate new feelings by adapting to my new life. Those initial ones seem to get pushed deeper and deeper inside. You reach a point where you can function at what is a new normal on the inside. On the outside you look as though you are moving on. This is what people see and it makes them feel that you are truly recovering from your loss.

But, I really don't feel like it's living. It's functioning. It's getting along. It's feeling okay. It's learning how to take care of yourself and getting used to living alone. I am all of those things. I am doing just fine. But, as I've said before, I know there's more. I've had "it".

I guess that makes me a romantic. Love at this age is different than at 16. It's more about companionship. About having someone to share your daily life with. It's about hugs. And it's about more than I have currently. And it's the scariest thing I've ever considered doing.

I bounce back and forth almost daily about what I want to do. But, if you know someone who's looking for an old gray haired farmer who likes to write stories, I may be available. Or not. Maybe. Not sure.......... You get the picture.

CHAPTER TWELVE

:

I BELIEVE

This chapter is definitely an opinion piece. My opinion. Developed over 50 years of attending church, Sunday school, Bible school and living life. I have heard many, many preachers, preach. I don't always agree with them. But, along the way I have certainly developed some ideas that I believe in. Religion can be very complicated. Religion is very personal. It is about your own relationship with God. I'm going to try and summarize and simplify my feelings about it. Not because you aren't smart enough to comprehend it but because I believe that lots of people try to overthink it. That makes it so much harder than I think God intended it to be. This chapter is what I believe and what I believe in. I've never really attempted to explain that. I think we may all learn something in the process.

First, I believe there is a God. And I believe He created each one of us. I believe that He only wants the best for all of us. I believe that He sacrificed His only Son, Jesus to pay for our sins.

Because we all sin. I also believe the Holy Spirit is God's voice and our conscience.

I believe there is a Heaven. I believe that it is a place without worry. Or fear. Or anger. I believe that it is a much better place than here. I believe that you cannot earn your way in. You can only get there if you believe in God and ask Him to forgive you for all your sins. Again, we all are sinners. We make bad choices based on greed and jealousy. I believe I will go to Heaven when I die. I believe that Mom is waiting there for us.

I believe there is a hell and that is where we will go if we don't believe. I believe that there are angels that watch over us. I believe that all children that die before the age of understanding, go to Heaven. But, I also believe that once you are old enough, you must believe to get there.

I believe that Christians don't do good things to get into Heaven. That won't work. Christians TRY to do good things because after you make the decision to believe in God, you Want to do good things. You also want to influence as many of your friends and family to believe so they will join you in Heaven. (This is especially true of your children) That's why Christians preach, write, sing, give children's sermons, bake things and have Thanksgiving dinners. Because we want to encourage people to be part of something much larger and longer than this life on earth. As I've said, we believe in Something we cannot see and Someone we cannot touch. I believe when I see sunsets, thunderstorms, babies, blue skies, growing corn, creeks that flood, and rain that falls. I believe because God gave me Mom. And all of you. And many friends. Who else could do that?

I believe our lives and our deaths serve some kind of purpose. That's why we aren't all born at the same time and die at the same time. I really don't know what that purpose is, unless it is to move God's kingdom along towards its final goal.

Why do I go to church? I need to. I admit that I sometimes make bad choices and think bad thoughts. I am not perfect. Neither was Mom. She was so special to us. But she was not perfect. We were just two people trying to make sense of life and wanted to be around other people who feel the same way as us. Can you be a Christian without attending church? Definitely. But, for me it would be even harder to do than it already is. I fail miserably at being a Christian sometimes. I need to be reminded, at least every Sunday about how to be better at that. I need that foundation of faith for when my life doesn't go well. Bad things will happen. Even to people who believe. We are humans with choices. That's what makes us different than animals. And we will make bad ones sometimes.

I believe we are born with an expiration date. Mom had one and I believe she somehow felt it was getting closer. That's why she worked so hard to be a Christian after she was laid off. I believe we are put here for a unique purpose but I'm not sure most of us know what that is. But, I also believe our friends and family may be able to understand what our purpose is much better than us.

I believe that it is the duty of every parent to lead by example and to encourage our children to believe in God. I want to make this very clear to you. I do not want to fail at this.

God gave us humans the ability to make our own choices. The ability to choose between right and wrong. I believe that God truly hopes that we will make the right choice but He will not stop us if we do not. Unless we ask him to. Through prayer. By simply having a conversation with Him.

How are we going to live during this journey? It's very clear how our life ends. We no longer exist. I believe the end is a fixed moment in time that we cannot change. What's not clear is how we are going to choose to live on the way there.

That's what I believe.

CHAPTER THIRTEEN

:

AN ANNIVERSARY

There is an important anniversary coming up soon. Sometime in late June or early July, last year, I purchased a stove. It's a really nice one. It goes really well with my other appliances. And it fits really well into the space reserved for it.

There is only one problem. I have never used it. I have never so much as boiled water with it. I'm not even sure I could even make it work. (I once tried baking some rolls with it but it kept shutting off)

I've been trying lately to figure out why I don't cook. I actually used to cook more than Mom. Simple things, of course, but I did do it.

Someone recently asked me if it was because I didn't want to fire up the stove for just one person. It really isn't very efficient to do that, they said. I agreed and quickly changed the subject because I truly didn't have an answer. I hadn't spent much time thinking about it. But now that I have, I think there may be a deeper reason.

I believe that I am angry. Possibly at God. That I have to cook for one. And that I have to eat alone. And that there is no one here to talk to while I cook. It may be my show of defiance against the situation I am in.

Anyway,

Happy Anniversary "stove"!

CHAPTER FOURTEEN

:

CHERIO!

Since I began writing Part Two of these letters I have struggled with trying to explain to you what I am missing in my life since losing Mom. I just haven't been able to describe my feelings to you in a way that satisfies me. But, recently I was looking at the UK news on my Kindle and stumbled on to a comment that perfectly summed up my problem. (I was looking at the UK news because my Kindle thinks I live there and none of you have been able to convince it otherwise).

Anyway, there was a short excerpt from a book written by a lady in Great Britain named Maddy Paxman. It is about the grief she experienced after losing her husband. He died suddenly of a brain hemorrhage at the young age of 50.

The comments she made were very familiar to me, including what she had to say about moving on after his death. (I have ordered the book to read). But she also said that she had heard many people make a certain comment about becoming a widower that I had never heard before. It was, "I have plenty of people to do things with, but no one to do nothing with". That really caught my attention!

I have lots of great friends and family. They, like you, have made me feel very welcome. I am truly blessed in that department.

What I don't have on a rainy afternoon or during a blizzard, is someone to do nothing with. THAT, guys, is exactly what I have been trying to explain to you that I miss the most!

The book is called "The Great Below: A Journey Into Loss" There may be nothing else in it that interests me or pertains to my situation. But, it really doesn't matter. That statement is the phrase that has eluded me in so many attempts at explaining to you what is missing in my life since losing Mom.

And for that I am truly grateful that you can't make my Kindle understand that I live in the US.

But, I am getting really tired of reading the inside scoop on all of the royal weddings.

CHAPTER FIFTEEN

:

ALL IN

I recently listened to a friend describe some of her escapades while teaching school on a Caribbean island. (She also lost her spouse at a young age) During one of her tales she somehow got sidetracked and got into berating her brother for thinking that just because he dated someone, he had to marry them. She said that was a small town, Midwestern, Presbyterian way of thinking.

I personally call people like that "all inners". I am one of those people if there ever was one. I met Mom, started "dating" her in junior high and never dated another woman until now. I wouldn't make a good "player". (As if you didn't know that). I have very conservative values and probably will not be able to overcome them and just date for fun. I actually wonder if that would be good for me at this stage of my life and mostly harmless. But, I probably won't do it. You see, I also believe if you put everything into a relationship that it takes to succeed, you won't have anything left for anyone else.

Yep, I'm an "all inner" for sure.

CHAPTER SIXTEEN

:

IT'S TOO FAR

Recently, I was talking to Bob and Megan about Maddy Paxman's book, "The Great Below: A Journey Into Loss" that I had read, about losing her husband. She had such a different perspective and different experiences than me. Even so, I was able to pull some similarities from the book that we both have shared. The comment about needing someone to do nothing with, and the fact that we agree that grieving for a loved one is never over, were two instances.

I believe that you probably adjust to grief and carry it and that person with you for the rest of your life. It just becomes another part of who you are and what you are made of.

The biggest difference in her book and mine is the way we approach telling a story. Being from two very different cultures probably has something to do with that. Megan, you once commented that a grief counselor you showed my writing to, said what I wrote was different than most because it was raw and unedited. I must admit that there is no premeditation to what I write. Something I am doing, or watching or hearing just triggers me to want to write down what I am feeling at that very moment. What I am thinking gets transferred to paper without a thought about who may like it or not like it. When I read it the next day or next month or even the next year, I often find that I no longer feel exactly that way. I may have changed, (probably), or I may have changed my point of view. But, I try not to mess with what I wrote so you will get an idea of just how I feel and how my life is changing and my progression through the process. Even though it is very tempting to do so.

For example, while writing about the "rawness" of my approach, I realized that I had one more comment to make that would finish my thoughts on the subject. But, I can't write that last line. It's too personal. Too much a part of me that I don't want to share, even though it would make the writing better or the idea more complete. (Some of you may think I've already shared too much☺).

It reminded me of another comment that grief counselor made after reading part one of this book. She said that she could tell that I was holding back "something" in several of the chapters. She said that I commented on a subject or a feeling just up to a point, then stopped without really sharing my deepest, and sometimes most important thoughts.

But, I sometimes just can't go that far. It's just too much. It's. Too far.

Until next year,

DAD

PART FOUR

of

LETTERS FROM HOME

"JUST SAYIN......."

:

Written from July 2014 to June 2015

Three and a half to four and a half years

after Mom passed

CHAPTER ONE

:

COMMUNICATIONS

It always amazes me to see what you guys pick out of my ramblings to talk about. Often, the things that I think are really important, you don't even want to discuss. And often, things that I believe to be relatively minor issues, you want to discuss at length. I suppose that shouldn't surprise me. When I read Maddy Paxman's book (The Great Below) about her grief journey, there were really only two things that struck me as being important to me. But, those two things were Very important in helping me to explain my feelings to you! We all seem to pull something different from our experiences.

I guess I should be happy that there is anything that I write that makes you laugh, cry or feel some other emotion. That is one of the main purposes in writing this. To instigate a response. To keep us communicating. I can't imagine what would happen to our family if we stopped talking about this journey. And I personally don't want to find out.

Just sayin.............

CHAPTER TWO

:

FORGIVENESS

Recently, I was reading part three over again and it struck me that I may not have explained the part about my cooking (the stove anniversary) as well as I should have. Actually, I may have just introduced more confusion into the subject causing you to question how you can be angry with God, but still love Him. (After all, He did take Mom from us at an early age). This is the one time that I am going to go against my practice of not editing what I have written. Not change it but add some further comments.

God made each and every one of us so He truly is our Heavenly Father. I believe He has broad shoulders so He can handle us being upset with Him. He knows that we don't understand all that there is to know about this world and our purpose here. It's truly a great thing that He has a tremendous amount of patience with us.

I am guessing that there have been plenty of times that you have been upset with me over the years. But, I also know from experience, that you still love me. Our relationship with God is much like it is with our earthly parents. We're not always happy with them, but we still love them.

Forgiveness is a gift from God. It is our way out. Or our way in. Forgiveness trumps anger and hate. And heals our hearts.

Maybe, it's time I started cooking again. Just sayin............

CHAPTER THREE

:

IT'S ON SALE!

I've been on a buying spree. I've been buying things that I have never had to purchase in my adult life. Mostly shirts. And shower curtains. And bathroom rugs. And a truck to drive on Sunday. And more shirts.

These things were always Mom's responsibility. (Maybe not the truck). She bought stuff and I wore it. I also hung it, applied it, drove it, and washed it. But she bought it. Or at least picked it out.

I truly didn't pay much attention to what colors, styles and brands were involved. But now I need to, and I need my house to look reasonably "okay". I knew she had relatively good taste so I simply retained the job of making things fit. Give me a big enough hammer and I can usually make things fit.

Anyway, last fall I decided that Mom's car was getting quite a few miles on it and it was time to trade it. But, what kind of car should I get? She always picked them out and it was my job to do the negotiating.

Ultimately, I bought another truck. I like trucks so why buy a car? I had a light colored truck. So I bought a black one. I at least knew enough to not buy a brown one. Then my trucks could not be seen together. Megan taught me to never mix black and brown. At least with clothing. So I assume the same goes for trucks.

Next, I moved to my upstairs bathroom. It only had a bathtub. No shower. Which meant that when all of the kids were home, everyone getting a shower before some function, could be iffy. "No problem, says I. I will add a shower to my bathtub". Just how hard can that be? (I have big hammers, remember)

Got that done. It only took twice as long and cost four times the amount budgeted. I found that if you throw enough money at a problem, it can be solved. Did I mention that the aforementioned bathroom is in the log cabin part of my house, built in 1856? And there are the original logs in there for walls?

Anyway, after finally getting the shower installed there were still many decisions to make. Such as; What kind of faucets, curtain rods, curtain liners, drawer knobs, light fixtures, bath rugs, towels and shower curtains should I purchase? These were a huge problem! Until I discovered............"online shopping sights". Did you know that you can sit at your computer and push some buttons and stuff will show up at your door? They even deliver to a guy that lives in the middle of a cornfield!

So why not order several sets of things in different colors so you can test drive them in your bathroom? And then make your decision based on just how they feel? Then you can't go wrong. Right? Except, I now have enough towels, rugs and curtains to last me out. Don't get me any of those items for Christmas. I am covered. For decades. I haven't figured out the return thing yet.

My next buying spree started in the spring. I had always purchased my work clothes but Mom picked out my dress clothes.

After she died I wore what I already had or clothes you guys gave me. So, I decided I needed some new shirts. But I hadn't really thought about what kind of shirts I liked. So I went to a department store. And after the allotted thirteen minutes of shopping, I found three nice shirts.

Feeling quite proud of my accomplishment, I took them home and hung them up. Until Sunday. On that morning I grabbed the shirt I liked the most off the hanger and pulled it on. Just barely. It was too small. So I got out another one. Same result. Didn't think the pastor would be impressed with me in a tube top so tried the last one. Nope.

I had made the assumption that because they were not made with cotton, like my work shirts, that I could wear a size smaller. Apparently shrinkage was not the only reason I needed a larger size. Apparently, rate of gain comes in to play also.

Anyway, I had purchased three shirts. None of them fit. So, I went back to the store to get the same shirts in the next size. But, of course they didn't have them. So, I went to the mall and guess what? They are having a shirt sale! I got five. Just in case. They all fit.

Now, I have a new problem. I have my class reunion coming up in August. How do I decide which shirt makes me look like I haven't gained any weight since high school? Mom usually made that call. But being a former holder of public office, I did what all politicians do when faced with a decision they don't want to make. I appointed a "shirt committee". Sort of a shirt "focus group". It was made up of the two friends I go out to eat with, and Megan. Problem is, they don't agree. I have been wearing my various shirts when I am with the focus groups and keeping track of their responses on a sticky note on the kitchen counter. Three shirts are tied for the lead.

I am not one step closer to knowing what shirt I should wear. But, I am the "decider". I will make my decision and live with it.

It's probably a really good thing that I didn't get the focus group involved in my boxer or brief decision. Just sayin……….

CHAPTER FOUR

:

FIRSTS

Lately, I seem to be on a run of doing new things that I have never done or changed since Mom died. I had hopes that these would slow down a little but I'm pretty certain that was an unrealistic wish on my part. This month seems to be filled with "firsts". And you all know how much I love constant changes in my life. Part of the reason that I fight them is because I have had so many to deal with since Mom's passing and part is just my personality. But, of course we don't really have a choice in the matter. I feel like God is peeling back my defenses like someone peeling an onion. One layer at a time. I think He's trying to find out who I really am and what I'm made of. Let's call it "the coming out of Dad".

I'm like a two year old throwing a temper tantrum as God drags me, kicking and screaming, into my new life. It won't always be pretty and I won't go quietly.

But, I bet it's entertaining for you to watch.

Just sayin...........

CHAPTER FIVE

:

CLASS REUNION

I previously mentioned my upcoming class reunion and my quest to find the right shirt to wear to it. Well, last Saturday it was held and I did attend. Actually, it was much more fun than I anticipated. My biggest worry beforehand was that I would not have much to visit about with people as most of my high school memories included Mom. We dated all through high school so I worried that discussing that time in my life would only serve to make me sad. I didn't really want to feel that. I also worried that people would be asking me about the events that led to her death. I especially didn't want to be reminded of that and wasn't sure what I would answer.

Ultimately, I managed to pacify most of my classmate's curiosity without going into a lot of detail and truly enjoyed seeing those that I hadn't seen in a long time. I didn't feel that just because we went to school together that everyone deserved a long emotional explanation. I felt that the ones who really cared were either at her funeral or at least contacted me back then. There was actually only one person who had the nerve to ask me if I was seeing anyone. Overall, though I had a really good time and handled it better than I thought I would. Once again, fear of the unknown turned out to be unfounded.

I did have reason to lack confidence at attending, besides having never gone to a reunion without Mom. The week before the reunion, Megan told me that she and Bob would come home so if I needed an excuse to leave early I could say I had company at home. I jokingly said that they couldn't come home that weekend because there would probably be plenty of ladies wanting to come back to my house that night. She was completely serious when she immediately responded, "And do what?" And then started laughing out loud. Boy, that's a confidence booster!

Anyway, the best part of the evening was that two women commented that they loved my shirt. Unfortunately, for the focus group, it was a shirt that I had picked up just a week before the event that no one had seen. That surely means that I can now totally rely on my own fashion judgement.

Here comes the white shoes and plaid pants!

Just sayin…………..

CHAPTER SIX

:

AN EXPERIENCE I HAD TO HAVE

Recently, I had the opportunity to meet with a grief counselor. I had never spoken to one since Mom died. I guess I never felt the need to. I am surrounded by an extremely loyal group of family and friends who I generally talk about my problems with. And I write letters. I have told you that writing is very therapeutic for me. And I talk to God. And Mom. They're also very good listeners.

Before I went to see this person, I was trying to figure out what it must be like to talk to a counselor. (I also was trying to figure out why I ever agreed to see her in the first place) Needless to say, I was very concerned about how it would work out.

Anyway, as more time passes since Mom's death, I find myself wondering where I am headed. Maybe she could help me figure that out? I also wanted to ask her what she thought about what I write. (I had sent her a copy before I went) I wanted to know if she felt what I wrote was helpful to anyone other than me. I know that you guys say that what I write is helpful to you but I was looking for an unbiased opinion. Would she validate the "letters" or tell me that I was making things worse?

I told you that lately I have been thinking about whether or not I wanted to go through the rest of my life alone. I also have wondered what kind of person I might be interested in having a relationship with. I didn't really plan on discussing those feelings with her, but when she brought up the subject of dating I found myself more than willing to talk about it. I came away realizing that I have definite ideas about what I want in that regard.

Overall, the visit was very helpful. We discussed a lot of subjects in an hour and a half. She made me feel extremely comfortable. I felt like I was talking to a close friend. She helped me to look at the whole picture when I was just looking at some of the pieces. She also encouraged me to continue writing letters to you. And to continue trying to explain to you how my life has changed.

Just sayin……………..

CHAPTER SEVEN

:

CHER BEARS

About a year ago, I finally agreed to getting rid of Mom's clothes. I have already written about the process and how hard it was for all of us. It represented more closure of Mom's life and death. I knew that Megan had saved back most of Mom's pajamas but I didn't know why. She had a bunch, as you know, because she really loved her flannels. And she loved putting them on after a hard day's work and relaxing on the veranda.

Megan called me back in April and asked if it was okay if she asked a friend of ours to make the pajamas into teddy bears. I thought that was a great idea so she made the arrangements and I took them over to her. We had no idea what they would look like or how many she might come up with.

Just before Thanksgiving, the lady called me to say that she needed to bring me the bears. She was running out of room in her dining room and there was not going to be any place to feed her family. I couldn't believe how many bears she had made. There were 24 in all.

I called Megan and told her we now needed to figure out how many to give away and to whom. This turned out to be much harder than we anticipated. At one point we even discussed keeping them all. Eventually, we decided to each make a list and compare them when we saw each other at Thanksgiving.

We were actually very close on our lists but decided to think on the last four for a little while longer. Finally we finished and agreed. We decided to give away eleven bears and keep thirteen. There were some that we just couldn't let go of. They represented a memory that each of us had that was just too personal and important to us.

If we had an endless supply, we would have given away more. Giving each bear away gave us the opportunity to show that person how much they meant to Mom. And how much we have appreciated the support of us and our family for the last four years.

We chose the right people to receive one. Based on their reactions, I have no doubt. When I started handing them out, I stayed and watched them open the package. It soon became apparent that I couldn't do that. It was too hard. I was giving away a very personal part of what we had with Mom. But, I still knew it was the right thing to do, so after the first two I just left them with people and told them to open it later. We received some of the most passionate responses that I have ever heard.

Those bears represent memories of Mom that I haven't thought of for a while. Memories that I will always carry with me.

Thank you Megan for a wonderful idea and for finding the "Cher Bear" stickers. They made them even more special.

Each bear was accompanied by a letter of explanation. Some were specially written but most were like the one on the next page.

"A CHER BEAR"

About a year ago, I finally agreed to getting rid of Cheryl's clothes. Megan had the idea of giving them to an organization that helps battered women get back into the workplace after leaving their husbands. In the process of bagging them up I noticed that she was separating the flannel pajamas into their own pile. I didn't ask her why as the job was already hard enough. Last spring she called and told me that she had held them back for another possible purpose. She wanted to know if she could have them made into teddy bears. I thought that was a great idea so she contacted our neighbor and friend, Jill, and made the arrangements.

As you probably already know Cher really, really loved a new pair of flannel pajamas. We wish we had more bears to hand out but we were obviously working with a limited supply. Jill took great care in making them by hand and did a great job. Megan and I spent many days agonizing over who to give them to. We hope they mean as much to you as each one means to us. And we hope you know how much you meant to Cher. We think each bear contains just a little bit of her spirit.

MERRY CHRISTMAS,

MEGAN AND BARRY

CHAPTER EIGHT

:

WHAT'S WRONG WITH ME?

Recently, I was having a discussion with a friend of mine about a mutual acquaintance who had just found out that they had cancer. It was a somewhat minor form (if that's possible) of cancer that could be cured completely with a very limited surgical procedure. My friend said that this person was making a big issue out of something that really wasn't. He said that he didn't have much sympathy for whiners who were just looking for attention.

My friend's family has had a really bad run on illness and death lately. They have had many tragic outcomes, including losing his wife, that have truly shaken his deep beliefs in a loving God. Yet, he had hardly spoken those words of criticism when he caught himself and apologized. He said, "I am so sorry. I consider myself a compassionate person but lately I find my first reaction to someone else's misfortune to be very calloused .Of all people, I should not be that way after what's happened to me and my family. I never used to be that way. What is wrong with me?"

I then told him a story of a bad accident that I stopped at. There was a large crowd gathered there. It was a single car accident involving two young men that missed a curve after a long night of drinking. I found myself making jokes about the cost of all the agencies being there to take them to the hospital to sober up. I truly didn't think they were hurt badly but later found out that one of them was seriously injured. I felt terrible. I also consider myself a caring person and wondered why and how I could make such inappropriate comments at the time.

Two persons suffering tragic losses. Two people whose first reaction to someone else's problems is a lack of sympathy. I believe it's not "what's wrong with us? It's what's happened to us?" And the way we respond. We don't feel that anything they have going on can possibly measure up to what we've been through. Our loss wasn't just an illness or an injury. It was final. It was the ultimate result. It was death and the loss that goes with it.

So, we throw up this wall that says, "Unless your wife, child or husband died, then you need to suck it up and quit whining. We didn't get the chance for our loved one to live, even if they would have not been in perfect health. You have no right to complain unless your loved one dies also".

Yes, we know better. We know it's the wrong response. We are really not that unsympathetic. Actually, we are very understanding of other people's problems as a result of what we've been through. I truly regret that life has done that to me. I didn't used to be that way. It makes me sad. And it makes me angry and determined to change that part of me. I will probably catch some grief about this chapter if someone outside the family reads this. But, it's the truth. And other widows and widowers have told me they have the same problem. And I am definitely not perfect.

Just sayin…………….

CHAPTER NINE

:

JUST NOT TODAY

(January 24th)

Today may be the day I dread the most every year. It is the day that, now distant memories tend to overcome what's right in front of me. It is the one day a year that I truly realize how inadequate I am for the task of living out this life without Mom. And for the task of being a father, grandfather and the person you all can discuss your problems with.

Each of you has had to make huge career decisions lately. And I find myself so wishing that Mom was here to help with that. I don't know that she would have any better answers. I don't know that she would tell you anything different than I have. But, at least I would have someone to talk to about it. We could give you answers that we had worked out between us. Someone would have my back. The one person in the world that had the same history as me, with you. Someone whose perspective came from very much the same place as mine. We would work it out between us and right or wrong, offer you our best advice. On this of all days, with

179

so much going on, I miss her. Maybe more than any time in the last four years.

I've told some friends that I have had two revelations lately. One, is that me and my generation are soon to be the "old guys". The generation above us is quickly leaving us. It seems I have spent way too much time attending funerals lately.

The second realization I've had is that nothing stays the same. There seems to be so many life changes for you and me lately, I can hardly keep up. When I was a boy, I felt that everything was constant and consistent in my world. Now it seems that Nothing is. Time marches on, as they say. And life is messy. It's not smooth. It's not a straight line on a graph. It zigs and it zags. A lot. Our family is in the middle of a large change in the direction of a zig. Or the zag. We can't lose focus. We have to remember the goal. To always support each other and our decisions. And to accept that we are all doing the best that we can. We will make mistakes. But, we will always work them out. That's what families do. Just don't ask me to have answers today. Because, on this day I don't have any.

I recently told Megan what I thought about someone not being there for her. I said, "It's hard to lean on someone who can barely stand themselves." That's where I am today. On this day you're going to have to go several steps higher for your answers. You'll have to talk to the Father that's at the top of the ladder. That's what I'm gonna do.

Just sayin……………..

CHAPTER TEN

:

IT'S THE CLIMB!

Recently, our pastor gave a sermon that really got me to thinking. (They all make me think but sometimes it seems he's preaching right to you) Anyway, the main theme of the sermon was to live life to its fullest every day. We never know when your time here on earth is done. The only thing we do know is that our lives, and those around us, are limited. (That expiration date thing again)

As you all know, I am not big on change. I'm sure that I am worse about that since mom died. It seems that there are so many changes forced on you after losing someone that I just wish the world would slow down. That's an issue that I have to try and work on every day. But, I also believe that there are certain events and people that it's good to hang on to. Let's call them "anchors". These are things and people that we can use as reference points to see how far we've come. They keep us grounded.

God, is the main anchor. My family and friends are anchors. So are traditions. Such as Christmas Eve services, Sunday church, spring planting, fall harvest, Pillsbury cinnamon rolls☺ and even our jobs. Having these constant people and happenings in our lives keeps us from losing our focus when the world spins out of control.

I know we are all going to die someday. I know we want to go to Heaven and be with God and Mom. That is the end goal. That sermon just reminded me that although I've lost my life partner, I still need to live my way to the end. I've told you that sometimes I feel like my life is very methodical and lacks passion. I often forget that it's the journey that's important. We shouldn't just sit here and wait for the end to come. Live your way there and it will be much more interesting. In the words of the popular Miley Cyrus song, "It's the climb"! ☺

Just sayin………………

CHAPTER ELEVEN

:

I WISH

I wish, as always, that you were still here.

I wish that you could see what our children have become.

I wish you could see how much their spouses mean to me.

I wish you could see our grandchildren.

I wish you could hear Grayson's laugh and see Gavin's smile.

I wish I could tell you about my good days.

I wish I could tell you about my bad days too.

I wish we could discuss the changes in our kid's lives.

I wish you knew how much I wish things were like they used to be.

I wish I could hear your laugh again.

I really, really wish I could get one of your hugs.

I wish you would tell me what to do about all the changes in my life and how you would handle them.

I wish that I didn't always have to be the responsible parent.

I wish you could assure me that you're okay.

I wish that you have found peace.

I wish you could see how much our family and friends have continued to support me.

I wish we would have had just a few moments before you left, so I could have told you some things.

I wish I could love someone else, but so far, I can't.

I wish that I could see you again.

Someday I will. It just can't possibly be soon enough.

Don't ever think that you are forgotten.

Just sayin…………..

Ps. I really, really miss you today and I have no idea why today any more than yesterday. I wish I knew the answer to that too.

CHAPTER TWELVE

:

ONE MORE WISH

It seems that there was one more wish that I failed to touch on in the last chapter. I wish that I could regain the enthusiasm for farming that I had when I first started. It's a struggle some days. That probably surprises you. I know it did me when I recently realized it. You see, I always thought my love of farming came from doing the job itself. I have always loved the smell of freshly plowed spring dirt and freshly mowed alfalfa hay. And I loved the challenge of planting seeds and watching them grow. I thought I loved this job because it was what I was meant to be. And I thought I loved it for the requirement of faith that it takes to do it. We throw thousands of dollars of seed and fertilizer out into the dirt and expect the good Lord to return us enough to cover that plus some kind of a living. I thought that was enough for me.

It turns out that all of those things are true, but there were some other reasons why I've been willing to take that risk. It seems that I was also doing it because I had a wife and then, kids to help support.

And I wanted them to be proud to say that I was her husband and their father.

Some days it is really hard to push through and to worry about the crops. Because, now I'm just doing it for me to make a living. I always thought that would be enough. Lately, I'm wishing I was also doing it for someone else.

Just sayin……………

CHAPTER THIRTEEN

:

IT'S OUT OF CONTROL!

It started as a simple phone call. And an innocent question. It's turned into a quest that sometimes consumes me.

I called Matt last February and asked what Gavin needed for his birthday. I often don't know what to buy so I wanted some guidance. "He needs a sandbox" said Matt. "I'll get one", said I. "Any particular kind? A frog sand box from the Toy store would work. I'll text you the website." Check. Gift idea covered. Until I received the text including a picture. A picture of a plastic sand box.

"That won't work", says I. These kids come from farm stock. Their father grew up in a cornfield. And he sells corn. Not to mention that their grandfather raises corn. So, I promptly changed the proceeding idea. Pronto! I decided to order up a genuine green and yellow sand box on line and have it delivered to my door. (Just like towels and curtains) Except, I could not find such a thing. I called in an expert. I called my John Deere tractor salesman who sells me everything John Deere green. He also failed.

So, I decided to build one. (It might be good to state that a plastic frog sand box could be purchased for $39.00.) And that was the beginning of the construction of Papa's Park.

You see my problem is that I have a kid's imagination, mixed with a farmer's fascination of John Deere stuff. And I have a charge account at the local John Deere dealership. This is costing me a fortune!

First there was what I called the basic "starter sand box". A simple yet sturdy and colorful testament to the correct color of farm equipment (in my opinion). Besides being green and yellow, it was also decorated with gold handles and an array of John Deere decals. (They cost more than the entire frog. Guess I should have asked when I ordered them!)

I was given certain limitations of width, length and height to fit in an exact spot. But while building it I realized I should have a sand box at my place for the little humans to play in. This would keep them occupied while we adults sat around the fire pit on the benches that I built two years ago.

And this sand box should look like a tractor. And I have practically no limitations on size because I have a two acre yard! But, how do you make such a thing? And just how large should it be?

I purchased two 4 by 8 ft. sheets of interior plywood and laid them out on the floor of my veranda. I also purchased a box of pencils and 4 large erasers. And for the next two weeks, every night I would sketch a different size and shape of tractor on the boards. I experimented until I felt I found the correct scale of the various parts. It took three erasers and 9 pencils.

The final product is 6 feet long and six and half feet tall. It weighs about 250 pounds. It looks a lot like one of my John Deere tractors. It has a lid to keep the critters out. (Once had a bad experience with cats and worms when Matt was young). And it has lights. Solar powered working lights. They come on every night. It took me one month of mostly nights to build and paint it. And it cost me a load of corn.

But, I had a great time building it. So, I kept going. Next, there was a green and yellow swing. Then a simple but large and very heavy picnic table. And the leftover wood produced a kid's picnic table. And finally, a fully trimmed out Cadillac version of a picnic table.

I should stop. I probably won't. I have sketches of 4 more park projects. The neighbors now drive by to see the new additions.

I wonder how big, a combine with a sand box base, a fort for a cab and a teeter totter for a soybean platform would have to be, to look correctly scaled? And how many loads of corn it would take to pay for it?

I may need a bigger yard,

Just sayin................

Until next year.

Dad

PART FIVE

of

LETTERS FROM HOME

"TIME TO GO?"

:

Written from July 2015 to December 2015

Four and a half years to Five years

after Mom passed

CHAPTER ONE

:

HISTORY

I hang out with a lot of different people. But, often I find myself out with a couple of widow ladies eating supper. We go out and discuss the latest issues we have encountered since losing our spouses. But we often complain about entirely opposite problems. They tend to complain about not being mechanically proficient. Plumbing, engines and tires cause them a lot of headaches.

I, on the other hand, face different challenges. I tell them that they can hire someone to fix their lawn mower or their leaky faucets. But I cannot hire someone to take care of one of my biggest worries. You see, I don't know the history of a lot of things in my house. And I don't know a lot of the facts regarding your childhoods.

I have many cabinets and cupboards full of knick knacks, pictures and "stuff" that I don't know who gave them to us or their significance. And I don't know facts, such as when you first walked and when you got your first tooth.

I believe that in most marriages women are the keepers of history. They are the preservers of memories and the keepsakes that go with them. Eventually, as you got older I can remember special events in your lives. But, when you were little, Mom did that. And she remembered your prom dress colors and who you took to your first dance.

I don't remember how old you were when you had the chicken pox or if you both even had them. And I don't remember if one of you always carried a high fever when you were sick. Anyway, you get the picture.

History. That's another thing we lost with Mom. I'd trade that knowledge for a broken water pipe any day.

Any day.

CHAPTER TWO

:

PAPA HAS RULES!

Soon after our first grandchild was born, I figured out that there were rules that needed to be laid down about Papa babysitting the small humans. After all, this is a democracy and the majority rules. And I am the majority at my house. My house, my rules! Right?

Plus, I was truly thinking of the children's welfare. It's not that Papa hasn't previously been closely involved in the raising of small humans. It's that Mom was here to advise and supervise me. Now, that's a problem.

I really believe that raising children comes naturally for most women. And for most men, it does not. I admit it. We must be trained by women. (In a lot of things, but that's another subject for another time).

A friend of mine once told me that you can rock any kid to sleep if you have a big enough rock. (He was joking!) That made me laugh but when I told it to my new bride, there was no laughter.

Only scorn. She looked at me like I had just run over her new puppy. I never told that joke in front of her again. Ever.

And then there was the 4th or 5th week of no sleep after our first born came to life. It seemed that sleeping more than a few minutes at a time was a concept that you didn't believe in, Megan. We were both exhausted. (The doctor finally agreed with this dumb farmer that she must be allergic to milk. AFTER she was six weeks old.)

Anyway, on this particular screaming session, it was my turn to get up with her when she awakened. Did I mention that she was in a bassinet about 3 feet from our bed? And it had wheels? And that I pushed her out into the hallway, shut the door and crawled back in bed?

Until the new mother realized what I had done. And all hell broke loose! I did not know that my lovely bride could pronounce some of the words that came out of her mouth. None of the explanations about Megan crying, no matter what I did, seemed to be worthy alternatives to what she would do to me if I didn't pick up the child immediately! Which I couldn't do fast enough.

So you can see why I am a little hesitant to be left with the small humans. It's not that I didn't eventually get trained into an adequate babysitter and father. It's my fear that the nightmares may return! The ones where the new mother is standing over me screaming, while her head spins on its shoulders. And she spews out obscenities at me. I'm not sure I can handle them again. They lasted for months.

But, I just got the call. The "sure could use your help watching the kids," call. I love my grandsons very much. But, Papa has rules! They have to be able to walk, talk and pee on their own. And though the oldest now qualifies, their parents are trying to slide the smallest one in on his cuteness alone. He certainly is cute but I'm not sure I should accept him. It sets a precedent. But, I probably will.

I can see it now. "Hey kids, let's go eat ice cream with sprinkles, in the combine while we drive around the yard! By then, the swimming pool I set up in the living room, should be done filling with water so we can turn the ceiling fan on high and make some waves to surf on! After that, we have to take the pony out of the kitchen back up to the neighbors, before they miss him."

But, then again, maybe we'll just get ice cream in town and circle the hospital parking lot. Just in case something happens. Better safe than sorry. I am truly unsupervised on this one. And my rules have been bypassed. I lay awake at night wondering when the exact moment was that I lost control of this situation.

CHAPTER THREE

:

THE ESSENCE OF MOM

This book has, and I'm sure will continue to start many conversations with all of you about Mom. There have been many questions answered, but the one that I don't feel I have gotten to the bottom of is, what made Mom special? Everyone believes their Mom to be special, and they are. But what do I think made Mom uniquely special to her friends and family? It has taken me a lot of writing and thinking, but I have finally arrived at my answer to that question.

It's very simple actually. Mom was not afraid to look silly and embarrass herself, in order to make the people around her feel good about themselves. When she was committed to something, it just didn't matter to her how she looked in promoting it. Her joy often just over rode the embarrassment, broke down people's defenses and made people want to get involved. Could I do that? Absolutely not. My reserved nature often prevents me from taking chances. But, maybe it's time I try.

Admitting how hard this journey has been, is very hard for me. And to tell these stories of my grief and how I have dealt with it, is completely out of character for me. I truly am going to need those "twenty seconds of insane courage and embarrassing bravery" (Part Two; Chapter Three) to allow others to read what I have written.

I hope you have gained some insight into how much my life has changed. Then my embarrassment will have been worth it.

CHAPTER FOUR

:

SEE YA LATER?

I have said that I started writing to help me move forward with life after losing Mom. And that it has been very therapeutic to tell the stories of how much my life has changed in the process. (I must admit that some of the chapters are just me telling you my opinion on something while I have a captive audience).

As the years have gone by, I have often wondered how or why I would end this part of the journey. I once thought that if I met someone special, that would end it. But, now I find myself concerned that I have done neither one. I haven't found someone, (of course I haven't really tried either) and I haven't finished the book. It's not that I think my life is about to end. But, I am project oriented and like to finish things. And most people would think that four years is enough time to write it.

So have I figured out exactly where I am going and if I'm going alone? No. But I have eliminated a lot of possibilities. And I now know I'll be okay no matter how this turns out.

After five years of losing Mom, someone seems to be pushing me to bring this part of the book and therefore, this part of my life, to a conclusion. I will probably still write letters but finishing this part seems to really be on my mind lately. It's as if she is telling me that I can't move forward until I finish it.

This book has given my family a reference or starting point for many discussions about Mom. About who she was and what happened to her. (Sometimes, before I started writing, I know you had questions but didn't know how to ask them or how to approach me.)

It seems to have answered at least some of those questions. I would not want to miss the hard but very beneficial sessions it's produced. They are what keeps us working through our grief.

Your perspective of what happened the day Mom passed was different than mine. Mostly, because you came into the situation near the end. You had missed the circumstances that had gotten us to that point. I believe that hearing the whole story, helped to explain why I made the decisions that I made.

I also think I have answered some of the questions about where Mom and I started and how we reached the point where you were old enough to remember our life together.

I talk about many of my issues of dealing with the loss of Mom. Many of them are just normal everyday problems. But, during the early stages of grief, everything seems BIG. At times the smallest changes in my life upset me, but they may not seem like much of a challenge to other widowers at all. We all respond differently to tragedy and diversity.

My grief forced me to focus on the issues that I write about in this book. Faith and hope forced me to conquer them again, even though I may have already done so earlier in my life. I have learned a lot about myself in the last five years. Don't feel sad for me when reading the sad parts. I don't necessarily feel the same way today. And if you really care about someone you've lost, you have to cross through sad to get to happy. It just means I'm on my way to a better place.

I'm really going to miss writing this. It took so long to write that it has become like a familiar old pair of shoes or your favorite pair of jeans. Whenever I was sad or whenever I found something funny, I would pull it out and write about what just happened. It's so bittersweet. I have loved doing it and yet I also knew it had to have an ending.

But, as Megan said at Mom's funeral, it's not goodbye. I'll see ya later. In the meantime, I'm going to try to get back to living so the first chapter, of the next book, can begin...............

LOVE YA,

DAD

PART SIX

WILL WE DIE OF A BROKEN HEART

OR GO FORWARD WITH A CRACKED ONE?

:

Written from January of 2016 to January of 2017

INTRODUCTION

In the recent hit Christian single, "Tell Your Heart to Beat Again,"* singer Danny Gokey tells us to pick ourselves back up after a tragic loss and move forward, "cause your story's far from over and your journey's just begun." Upon hearing the song on the radio, several of my friends called or texted to say that I should listen to it. (I guess they were trying to give me a little "push".) I was already a fan of his and recalled hearing the song but hadn't paid close attention to the words. After doing so, I felt like many others that it was almost written for me. About my life story. And my new relationship. (Recently my friend and I were lucky enough to get to hear him perform the song live.) The lyrics assure us that the empty feelings don't have to stay with us forever.

It has become, "our song".

*Off Danny Gokey's 2014 album titled "Hope in Front of Me" written by Matthew West, Randy Phillips and Bernie Herms

CHAPTER ONE

:

FULL CIRCLE

When I finished "LETTERS FROM HOME: I Loved Ya Before I Even Met Ya" I felt I had exhausted all of the stories that related to my journey of grief. We lost Mom in January of 2011. I published the first edition of this book in January of 2016. I stated then that I always felt I would end my writing when I found someone new. Someone who could change the life path that I had been on for the last 5 years. But that just didn't seem to be in the cards. I wasn't getting any younger so I went ahead and released the book. My life was basically good but it was lacking passion and had become somewhat methodical.

Well once again, I was wrong. Wrong about so many things. Wrong about where I should end this story. And wrong about the cast of characters who were going to join me on the rest of this journey. (Actually, one character and her supporting cast in particular.) For shortly after I published the book my life took a dramatic turn. I had not anticipated this when I took charge of the proceedings. As usual my lack of faith and my determination to control where I was headed were proven totally off base. It seems that God once again had plans for me that differed from mine. So He stepped in and put into motion the events that would place two lost souls on a collision course. A course that brought us together when we least expected it. As you know, I have started seeing someone. "Courting" her even. And I started writing what I thought was a second book about the trials of starting a new relationship at age 60. But lately I realized that what I was writing was actually the true ending for the first edition. "Letters Fron Home" was originally five parts that began with me falling in love for the very first time in my life. Most of those first five parts are about loss. At that time (January 2016) loss was really all that I had experienced. I not only lost Mom but I lost the only life I had ever known since I was a teenager.

Now though , I am experiencing the complete opposite. The part most of us widowers won't allow ourselves to believe possible. The good side of a grief journey. The side where you find someone again. Someone who not only meets the criteria that I laid out in Part Two but exceeds them in every way. I am definitely doing better than I deserve (as my pastor says). I've found someone who understands how I feel and knows what I've been through because she's been through it also. Someone who needs me. Someone who I need. And someone who accepts this old, gray haired farmer for what he is and with no intention of trying to change me.

So here I go again. Adding to those same stories of grief but with a totally different perspective. Now it is a story of hope and anticipation for the future. In this Part Six I will explore the major changes that have sometimes overwhelmed me lately. Many of them caused by the progression of my grief journey. And many caused by the very act of releasing the first edition of Letters From Home. Life seemingly continues to come in waves for me.

I once felt I had run out of stories to tell. Of letters to send. But lately I've found I need to keep my children informed of my life changes maybe now more than anytime since losing your mother. Those changes have not slowed at all. In fact they have accelerated at an alarming rate. They are having a huge impact on you. And on her children. I've come full circle. I started this story by falling in love with a girl. For the first time in five years it seems almost possible now that it could end that way also.

CHAPTER TWO

:

STORIES

We all have a unique life story. And if you have lived into middle age the chances are high that you also have a grief story. A story of loss and how it affected you. I've received many letters, e-mails, texts and phone calls since releasing the first version of my book. Amazing and humbling responses. It seems that after reading about my loss and my continuing grief story people want to tell me theirs.

Those stories have touched me in a way that I did not anticipate. They made me laugh and they made me cry. Many have shared their personal journeys. I've felt we instantly have a bond. Although each story may not be exactly the same, the outcome ultimately is.

As I've mentioned before, I had no intention of letting anyone other than my children read these letters. I felt they were just too personal. And that I would be giving away what was left of my heart after losing Mom. They were simply some thoughts and feelings it seemed you should know. Thoughts that included the history of Mom and I and the huge impact losing her had on my life.

I was deeply worried about releasing the book. Not just to the public in general but also to my local church family. I've had a fragile existence at our church since she passed.(Because of my lack of confidence, not because of how I've been treated.) Together we spent so many good times there. It's been very hard to return and find my way and where I fit. One of the toughest mental and emotional battles I have faced. We just never know how grief is going to effect us. Over time I seemed to have found where I can still make an impact and yet not feel so out of place. I really didn't want to mess that up by releasing my book and possibly changing people's views and expectations of me.

I also struggled with letting my closest friends and family see what I wrote. Most of them had no idea I had a need for recording what had changed in my life and were completely caught off guard when I released it. One of my best friends even joked that he didn't know that I could read yet alone write in complete sentences! I spent a lot of time discussing my plans with my immediate family before going ahead with this project. In the end I grudgingly allowed it to be seen and have not regretted it at all. It has seriously expanded my circle of friends and is definitely responsible for my new relationship. I believe it has also given me more confidence to move my life forward. Which in turn has encouraged my children to make moves in their lives they had seemingly put on hold.

Les Brown, a respected motivational speaker and author once said we should, "make the reason for moving forward in your life bigger than you and larger than what you are going through at this moment." I often refer to myself as "the accidental author". I didn't begin this project with publication as the goal. It seemed it was time I followed the advice I had often given my children. I've said if you give something away from your heart, it will be returned to you many times over. It's hard for me to not be under the radar. I've learned from the many responses that reading about my grief journey lets people know that someone else has had the same feelings and thoughts as them. I am inspired and blessed. And I am truly selfish. I want and I need to hear their stories also. Every one of them. So I will once again put my personal experiences out to be seen in this revised edition. Stories within the overall picture that I hope move it forward. Stories that are real. My wish is they have some content that people facing their own grief can relate to. With a new part that proves that there is hope in this journey, not just loss. And with the selfish wish that I receive more responses in return. I truly believe somehow God gives me the ideas and Mom gives me the motivation to share them. I know that statement may be very presumptous of me but I simply do not feel I could have looked forward and dreamed these letters would be something that others would relate to. I've also come to believe in a statement by Martin Luther who once said, "If the Holy Spirit should come and begin to preach in your heart, giving you rich and enlightened thoughts….. be quiet and listen to Him who can talk better than you; and note what he proclaims and write it down". Not long ago it was pointed out to me by another widower that as Christians and as someone who has been on this journey for a while, we have an obligation to pass on what we have already learned and experienced. To possibly help those who have not started or who have just started down this path.

A lady recently sent me a note in response to reading the original version of my book. In it she seemed to have focused in on the parts where I had commented that I felt ill-prepared to handle life after Mom. In it she reminded me, "God does not call the equipped. He equips the called!" It's that kind of reinforcement that keeps me telling stories.

CHAPTER THREE

:

THE LAST PIECE or THE LAST PEACE?

Three months after Mom died, on a road trip for groceries(remember I live 15 miles from the nearest town of any size), my daughter turned to me and asked this question. "Dad, do you think you'll ever be happy again?" I replied, "I sure hope so because I would hate to think I was going to feel like this for the rest of my life."

I lost a huge piece of my heart when I lost Mom. I felt I gave away another piece when I released my book to the public. I've often wondered just how many pieces I had left, if any. Regarding that subject, the following story is a summary of the most recent monumental changes in the life that is called, Barry.

It began with a text. A simple request to meet and discuss my book about losing Cheryl. She was nearby mowing her mother's yard and wondered if I would have time for her to drop by and compare how closely her grief journey paralleled mine. We'd known each other for over fifty years. We'd grown up almost exactly one mile apart (which to country folks is like being next door neighbors). I knew her parents well. I had done business with them many years at their shop. Recently her mother and I attended the same church. But this lady was in my brother's class. Two years older than I. Practically ancient in grade school years. We'd never really hung out together.

She had married after college and moved away from our community. I married and stayed. Occasionally we would run into each other and say hi. We were happy with our choices and made new lives. Lives we both loved with people we loved.

Now fast forward to that fateful and innocent meeting. It lasted more than four hours! We did not move from our seats. We did not drink. I didn't even offer her chicken. I didn't offer her so much as a glass of water. We just talked. Easily and openly and oh so comfortably. For four hours. I'm sure that was more words than we had spoken to each other in our lifetimes. Then she returned to her home 35 miles away.

My daughter was extremely upset with me when later that evening I relayed the details of our encounter. She scolded me for being such a poor host. I must admit my experience at hosting cute blondes in the last five years is rather limited. Well, very limited actually. (The two cute blondes that I often go out to eat with will probably abuse me for that comment.)

"You should apologize " Megan screamed. "Your reputation in the community of Bald Bluff will be tarnished forever !" she cried. And so that very night I immediately did what any responsible 6th grader would do. I sent her a text. Yep. Not a misprint. I am almost 60 years old and I sent my apology in a text. (Smooth, right?)

In the text I sincerely and profusely asked for forgiveness for what my daughter so forcefully pointed out was complete and utter stupidity on my part. I also offered (that was my idea) to make it up to her. I stated (in my 6th grade text) that I would be honored if she would select any place in the world (almost) she would enjoy eating dinner and I would be happy to deliver her to such location at a time of her choosing. And I would pick up all of the forthcoming costs and expenses associated with this endeavor to correct my many mistakes during the previous visit.(Really smooth !)

One long week later arrangements were made (through several texts). I would meet her in the Target parking lot. She was going to be nearby. And we would begin our harmless adventure to appease my guilty concience.

There it is. Our first "official" meeting. Set up entirely through texting. (Which cost me another beat down by my daughter.) We talked for hours. The staff informed us they were closing. I delivered my charge back to Target. "I have truly enjoyed the evening" said I. She replied the same. I also added that if she would ever have the need to partake in some more edible swallowing and conversating to let me know (through a text of course). And I would promptly return to the big city again. And the Target parking lot. No pressure. No expectations. Just another dinner if she were ever hungry in the next 20 years or so. (Super smooth!) I drove back to my house in the cornfield where I live. Wondering what had just happened. Or if I would ever hear from her again. With a crack in my armor and an ache in my heart that I couldn't get rid of.

And three days later...............

A text came through.

And a new journey began.

But,

"Go slow ," my friend said.

"Don't let her get too close!"

"Your heart has been broken once before."

"Throw up that boundary and turn down that charm !"(Hey, its my story.)

"Hold something back."

"And go really, really slow."

"But, above all else, don't let her have that last piece of your heart."

"It may be all you have left !"

And three weeks later,

She had slipped in the back door to my heart.

She got by all my defenses.

I cannot sleep.

I'm not hungry(not even for chicken).

I feel like I'm 16 again.

I'm scared and excited at the same time.

I need to hear her voice.

I need to hold her hand.

I need a hug.

My passionless, methodical life has been changed forever.

Even if this doesn't last forever.

I am alive again.

Like a "thief in the night" she's doing what I was supposed to guard against.

She is slowly, but surely stealing what's left of my heart and I don't know how to stop her.

And I really don't want to.

In the three shortest weeks known to mankind, I've let her take what may be the last piece.

Or is it the last peace ?

I am in so much trouble here !

"No risk, no reward Papa", my daughter-in-law reminded me. (With a smirk on her face.)

"And oh what a ride it will be, said I."

"And oh what a ride it will be!"

Note: Recently, I was talking to a trusted friend of mine when I worried out loud at how quickly the new blond had stolen my heart. He wisely replied, "Barry, for you I feel it's not been just three weeks. Really, it has been 5 years and three weeks. I say you just go with it and see where it takes you." Thank you Tom. You don't know how much I needed to hear that.

CHAPTER FOUR

:

LET'S DANCE

"Until you get comfortable with being alone you'll never know if you're choosing someone out of love or lonliness." Mandy Hale

I've made another discovery in the life that's called Barry. You see, because of recent developements I have realized how lonely my life had become and that I had somehow grown to believe that was okay. I just didn't feel that I would matter again. And be the center of someone's life again. Until I found someone "to do nothing with" I didn't feel that would ever change.

Before losing Mom I felt I had it all. A life filled with wonderful family and friends. I hoped someday to find that again. I had very little confidence I would. I was yearning for not just one piece of the puzzle but for the whole picture. All of the pieces. Together at the same time. Who gets to have that once in a lifetime let alone twice? Why would God grant such a wish to me such a poor keeper of his promises?

Looking back I now realized just how much I had taken for granted. Those things which I now miss the most. I had especially forgotten that my wife and our marriage were a gift. And I had forgotten we are given a specific number of days on this earth to enjoy and bring joy to those around us. I am ashamed I had lapsed into believing I had earned that life. And for that I am deeply sorry.

This new relationship is the next step in my grief journey. It is and will continue to be complicated and littered with challenges. We are both acutely aware of that. But, I do want it all. And I've found someone who wants the same thing. It would have been so much easier to have stayed on my own and not jumped off the cliff into the unknown. That's what I would have done before Mom died. I would have played it safe. I would have taken the easiest course. I'm not that person anymore. I'm going for a two-fer. Two wonderful relationships in one lifetime. An endeavor destined to fail miserably? Or did God bring us together to prove to all who are watching there is yet another special person for us? Even at this age? Who still has so much to give and to share? And even though he has taken our first love, he has provided us with another chance. If we just have the faith to use the "20 seconds of courage and embarrassing bravery" that I talked about in Part Two. (from the book "We Bought A Zoo")

We also realize we have a 50/50 chance of one of us having to bury another person that we've allowed ourselves to fall in love with. The alternative is to live out our life alone. I could do that. I have done that for over five years. I have weighed the risks.

And I think I'll dance.

CHAPTER FIVE

:

ONLY TWO WAYS TO GO?

I've been in several discussions lately on the topic of which way is harder on us to lose a loved one. It's not a pleasant subject but it seems to come up occasionally among the widowers I hang out with. So which is worse? The sudden , tramatic loss when you are not expecting it? Or the loss of a loved one to an extended illness?

I've experienced the first one with my wife. I've told how ill-prepared I was. I've discussed my deep regret at not having the chance to tell her how much I admired her and how much she meant to me. And the complete and utter shock I experienced for more than a year.

Is that any worse than watching your loved one die slowly? In that scenario you probably get some time to speak the words you want them to hear. You get to somewhat prepare yourself for what's to come (if there is such a thing as being prepared). But the person who is leaving you slowly may be one of the most important in your life. Over time they may be changing into someone totally different than the person you once knew. Both physically and emotionally. How can that possibly be a better alternative to a sudden loss?

Why is there a difference in the first place? Why would God have two completely different scenarios for us to witness with basically the same inevitable outcome? What possible purpose does either serve? And why do some of us leave this earth so young while others live a long and full life?

So many questions with so few satisfying answers. We humans like to think if we just study every word and idea we will acquire those answers. We are sure there is nothing we can't uncover if we put our minds to it. I suggest we won't truly discover the answer to some of life's mysteries until we pass on and get to Heaven. Because as humans we simply do not have the capacity to comprehend all that is happening here on earth or in Heaven.

And that might be a good thing. At least for me. I'm also not sure I have the ability to handle those answers anyway.

CHAPTER SIX

:

GOD WINKS

I recently attended a gathering where several people recounted their stories of how they felt God or their passed loved one gave them a sign they were doing well and were safe in their surroundings. Many spoke of how that sign gave them tremendous comfort. For a time I was extremely jealous. I have never felt I received any personal confirmation like that. I've often wondered if He or Mom had sent me one but that I was not capable of recognizing it. Finally , after five plus years I just gave up on the idea and moved forward.

That night as I listened to each one tell their story, I did realize something else. Mom often told me while she was alive, that she knew she was going to Heaven. She believed with all her heart that she would have a better life than she had here. She was excited about that. She had no doubts. I received my "God wink" while she was still here. Directly from her. Before she ever passed she made it very clear. I just needed to have faith to believe what I'd already been told. Once again, my problem. Not His. It always seems to come back to me.

CHAPTER SEVEN

:

A SMALL HUMAN EXPERIENCE

I actually baby-sat the small humans last week. All alone I kept track of the grandchildren. Why is this such an important milestone? As I explained in Part Five, my confidence in many things since losing Mom has been severely shaken. Including my ability to be responsible for the small humans by myself. Before , I always knew I had a backup if I needed help. Now it's one more project I often must complete alone. I survived and so did they. Although at times I wasn't sure that would be the final outcome. As the night wore on I realized that was the goal. The only goal. At least for me.

My children lied though. They said they would only be gone for four or five hours. That turned into seven. Then eight. And finally nine long hours !

The small humans and I participated in every activity I had planned. In the first thirty minutes ! We played in the sandbox. We kicked the ball. We went "willy" high in the swings (them more than me). We mowed the yard with the obnoxious, fake lawn mowers (only because we couldn't get the real one started). We even chased the dog until some of us were out of breath.

We drank juice boxes. We ate snacks. We played some kind of game that I'm sure the 4 year old was cheating at. And we were forced to rest for only 15 minutes of the 30. "Now what should we do?" asked Papa. (I decided it was my turn to ask the questions) I considered calling their mother for suggestions but decided that would make me look incompetent. I was all out of entertainment ideas.

Then it hit me! We could fall back on that ground breaking, technological invention of the twentieth century. We could turn on the television! If we only knew which of the four remotes, with their 28 buttons each (I counted) would achieve the aforementioned result. "No problem Papa" said the four year old. "G2 knows how!"(he's three).

So, for the next 2 hours "we" were glued to the TV. Specifically, the Disney channel. With repetitive shows about some kind of robotic creatures. I was assured they were the good guys. With the most power. Hard to imagine that Papa needed that clarification. About 17 times. I'm not exactly sure as I stopped counting after the seventh reminder from the four year old.

"Sleepy time" finally arrived at 8 o'clock. This was the time their parents insisted I begin the process by which every attempt be made, to enforce all of the procedures needed to wind the super charged motors running in the small humans down to zero. (I'm serious. The parents of the little ones actually spewed out something that sounded a lot like that!)

There were jammies to pull over bodies in perpetual motion. And potty visits. And something that appeared similar to brushing of "toofes". And books to read. Which caused arguments to ensue about which small human's turn it was to choose their favorite story. (Papa finally intervened after realizing that no one was going to be happy regardless of the decision.) At least two and a half "dwinks" of water were then deemed appropriate and one more potty break, "just to make sure". And they were finally, blissfully in bed. Not asleep. That took about 40 more minutes and more returns upstairs by Papa to answer questions. At least they were in the designated slumber areas that had been alloted to them by their parents. Mission accomplished !

During that evening I actually believe I gained three neighbor kids, a couple of dogs and one cat. After recognizing the increase in body count I was going to choose some to send home. But being the highly skilled and intelligent sitter that I am, I decided to let them stay until bedtime. That way I had some replacements in case one of the "originals" came up missing. I was sure that I started with 4 small humans. When I mentioned that fact to their parents upon their arrival, they quickly responded that I only had two !

Wow! It sure seemed like there were more than that...........

CHAPTER EIGHT

:

A SECOND CHANCE?

The discussion was about finding your "soul mate". It began before I arrived at the restaurant. When I sat down at the table I was immediately asked if I felt I had found mine when I found my wife. Or if I thought it was even possible to find the one person on this earth that was an exact fit with your soul? I responded without hesitation, that I had no doubt that Cheryl was that person for me. Someone who was not perfect but was perfect for me at that very moment in my life. And she would have always been that person had she and I lived to be 100. This discussion reminded me of a comment I recently saw posted on Facebook. It said, "When a man truly loves a woman, she becomes his weakness. And when a woman truly loves a man, he becomes her strength. This is called an exchange of power."(Gentleman Rules) Kinda sums up the way I felt about our marriage. We were all in, together.

Mom died at the young age of 54. Five long years later I've found someone to begin a new relationship with. And when you start a new relationship you get a chance to be the person you may have always wanted to be. Before you fell into the mold your previous life and circumstances created for you. You get to make changes that you may have regretted not making sooner. I realize you can't take back or cover up a lifetime of living so you basically are what you are by now. I don't believe you get to totally reinvent yourself. But that doesn't mean you can't use what you've learned and experienced in life to make what you feel are some improvements.

You need to understand that Mom was definitely my soulmate for as long as she lived. But with her loss, I believe there may actually be another person out there who fills the void in my heart. It's taken me a long time to truly believe that. In other words, different soulmates for different stages in your life. Again, someone who is not perfect but is perfect for me at this particular moment in time.

The thought has actually crossed my mind that I may not even be Mom's "person" now, if we were meeting for the very first time. Because I have changed, a lot. Losing her has had a profound effect on me. I'm not the same person in many ways. So maybe I wouldn't even be her soulmate after what life has done to me. Just the act of writing this makes me very sad. Then again, maybe this is my opportunity to try and do it better. Maybe this truly is my second chance ?

CHAPTER NINE

:

DEAR CHERYL

Recently I was listening to a friend of mine describe the first edition of this book to another lady who had not read it. I was letting her tell the story because I was interested in hearing her take on it. I find that people's response to what I write varies greatly and they sometimes focus on something totally different than what I was trying to emphasize. My friend stated in her review that, "it is written in the form of letters to his children." The listener caught me completely off guard when she turned to me and asked, "Why aren't they written to your wife? Are any of them written to her?" I replied, "No, they are all written to my kids." (Actually you could say the the chapter in Part Four, "I Wish" is addressed to Cheryl but my intention was to explain my feelings to my children.) I'd previously thought about designating one chapter to her but wasn't sure that anything I would put in that chapter would be useable here. I questioned if I could write something that would express my feelings but not go so far as to tread into the deeply personal ground that I feel I have so far avoided.

Her question made me consider this subject once again and reminded me of a story I heard. It was about a woman who lost her spouse suddenly in an accident. She still had young children at home and had not worked outside the home for many years while raising them. Her grief counselor asked her if she was angry at her husband for leaving her in such a mess? Until that time she had not considered that she might be upset with him. She was probably so busy just trying to survive that she hadn't had time to consider that. After the counselor brought up the idea she realized that she did harbor some feelings of abandonment along with the feelings of grief associated with losing him. Her counselor encouraged her to write a letter to her deceased husband expressing those feelings as part of the healing process. So with that story on my mind and the push from my friend, I will attempt to do the same.

Dear Cheryl,

I do sometimes wish that you were here and I was in Heaven. The struggles of moving forward without you are often more than I feel I am able to handle. Losing you as my wife and also my best friend left me very vulnerable and in a place I've never been. You see, I lost you without having You to help me through it. Which is what you always did when I needed support. This is indeed the most devastating part of this journey and what has had the biggest impact on who I am now and how I react to change.

I realize now I not only loved you but had also come to admire the person you became. For what you had done with your life and how you lived it. I deeply regret that I took you for granted. And more specifically I regret that I often told you "no". Not no to more things but no to chances to spend more time with you. Precious time that I'll never get back. Doing the little things that were important to you. And now have become so important to me. I loved and miss every part of you. Even the parts that weren't perfect. At least those parts were mine for a little while.

I'll never forget,
Bear

P.S. I've met a girl. Yep, a real life lady. And after several months, for some reason she's still hanging around. Listening to my stories. And laughing at my jokes. Can you believe that? You would like her. I know that's true because you already told me you did. A long time ago. So I have one more favor to ask of you. Can you please let me know when I'm messing up this new relationship? Just a subtle reminder would be good. I still need that from you.

CHAPTER TEN

:

AMEN!

I must start this chapter with an apology. And by asking for the forgiveness of my church family and my pastor. And by telling them just how grateful I am for their continued support of me and my family on our grief journey. I really do appreciate all they have done. But……..

It had been an emotional week. With many trying days and exhausting nights. So when I arrived at church on Sunday morning I was in a mood that is hard to describe. I had been dealing with several stressful situations that week and needed some relief. Not necessarily a good place to be while sitting in a quiet sanctuary listening to our pastor speak of serious life matters. I was trying to concentrate but then the collection plate was passed. And my focus diminished. Well, actually it left the building.

I was sitting with my cousin and his daughter. (We'll just refer to her as "Cassie" so she can remain anonymous.) Three seats over and one row in front of me was a close friend I've known my whole life. We usually go out to eat together at least once a week when he and his wife and son allow me to tag along on their family dinners.

For historical background purposes you also need to know that my cousin has three great kids and a wonderful wife. And that I have leaned on them heavily since losing Cheryl. And starting several years before the "incident" I had been known to give each of the children a small amount of money to put in the collection plate before it arrived in our pew.

So as the plate was being passed I reached into my pocket and all I could quickly grab besides my weekly donation was 27 cents. I handed it to Cassie(alias) . No problem. Except my friend in the row ahead and three seats over witnessed the action. And he put his hand out and whispered the words, "What about me?"

Reaching back into my pocket, all I found was a lonely penny so I passed it to Cassie. Who passed it to her dad(my cousin) and finally to my friend ("George" from now forward). That should have been the end of this story. Unfotunately, it was not. For a few minutes later, Cassie handed me a church bulletin with writing on it and a dime. At the bottom of the front page had been written(by George) the following statement. "For those who give generously, He will repay them ten-fold."

I smiled. Cassie smirked. Her dad laughed out loud. And George grinned with the satisfaction of believing he had won the game. And one would think this would have been a good place for two sixty year olds to stop playing and pay attention to the preacher. Not so. I love a challenge. I reached into my billfold and pulled out the last bill in it which was my lucky one hundred dollar bill. I passed it to Cassie. Who gave it to her dad. Who was struggling to keep his composure but managed to pass it on to George. He examined it carefully, smiled at me and promptly stuffed it into his pocket while mouthing the words, "Thank you".

After a few minutes my money returned as Cassie and her dad continued to restrain their laughter while watching the proceedings. Not wanting to give up on my hopes of increasing the ten-fold return on my investment, I then sent my credit card through the process(with the information that it had a $5000 limit.) After receiving it George simply turned his attention back to the pastor. End of story? Nope. Another missed opportunity to end the nonsense was bi-passed when my credit card returned, with a gift card to a tool store.

By now the pastor was deep into the sermon and probably wondering which children were causing all the rukus in the back row of the back room. I felt it was time to end the ever escalating series of events (which some would say I started but I totally deny that accusation). So I handed Cassie my FOID card (Firearm Owners Identification Card) with this verbal message, "Tell him to go buy a gun of his choice and use it to threaten himself if he can't write a two page summary of the sermon at the end of the service!"

My cousin and Cassie turned beet red while delivering the final message. George didn't look my way again until we were singing the closing song. And only after we were dismissed did he utter the words I really wanted to hear when he asked, "Where we going for lunch?"

Why am I telling you this story which clearly isn't behavior of which I am proud? What does this have to do with my grief journey? As they say, nothing and everything. You see, grief tends to suck the joy out of every situation. Even the good ones. It just sneaks up on you when you think you've moved forward. You never know what will trigger the often overwhelming surge of emotions. A picture, a sound or a smell, a phrase or just a single word can be the cause. And it often leaves you full of raw and angry emotions that bleed into every facet of your daily life. With the week I had just been through, my normal tendency in the last five years would have been to crawl back inside myself. To hold in my frustrations and suffer through it. By the grace of God I believe I have turned the corner. I have a new attitude since finding someone I feel I can say almost anything to. An outlet for those frustrations with a person who accepts my many faults. And the belief that it's okay to relax and enjoy life again. And not be perfect doing it. I'm just so sorry Pastor, that you had to bear the brunt of my bad week and be a witness to my shenanigans. I promise I'll try to be better next Sunday. But he started it !

CHAPTER ELEVEN

:

LOST LOVED ONES

The next two chapters are about issues so important for you to know and understand that I'm not going to elaborate on the topics for fear of diluting their significance. I have mentioned them in previuos chapters but now feel the need to point them out. They deserve that much of your attention.

My friend and I speak freely and openly about almost everything that has happened in our past lives. That is literally how our relationship began. And one of the most important aspects of our discussions is that we find it extremely easy to discuss our lost spouses in front of each other. We often find ourselves referring to them when we talk. Not all previously married couples can do this. There is truly no jealousy and no resentment from either of us.

We both loved our spouses and intended to stay with them until one of us died. And unfortunately that happened. Way before we were ready. We will never stop speaking their names when memories invade our thoughts. Without the freedom to do this we just don't believe our relationship would work.

CHAPTER TWELVE

:

NOT ENOUGH TIME

We are aware that our families don't believe we have as much time for them as we used to. Our friends say they hardly see us anymore. Some don't believe I have a lady friend or that she actually exists. Some have even gone as far as to joke that she must be an "imaginary friend."

We've each spent the last few years trying to fill in the time we used to spend with our spouses. When you lose someone you have to account for each and every minute spent with them. So you begin to fill those voids in your life by building an entirely new set of habits and activities. We are now trying to do that all over again with each other instead of seperately.

How do we work out the fact that at sixty years old we are both deeply embedded in our families, churches and communities? And we live 35 miles apart. The logistics and time management are daunting!

We have to constantly work at alloting our time between each other's families and friends in a "fair split". When we look at our combined weekly itinerary , it is amazing to us just how little time we have available to spend alone together. It often doesn't afford us the time we feel we need. Time to just hang out and get to know each other. And time to do nothing, together.

We are both seriously aware of what happens when one of you quickly runs out of time (Her husband passed suddenly at an early age.) In Proverbs 16:9 it says, "the human mind plans the way but the Lord directs the steps." A reminder that God was fully aware of the many challenges we would face to make this relationship work when He "threw" us together. I don't know if we'll succeed but I'm counting on him to lead the way. Which will surely improve our chances. So please be patient kids! This is hard!

CHAPTER THIRTEEN

:

NO REGRETS

In a previous chapter I noted that one of the biggest worries I've had about starting a new relationship is the fact that it is likely one of us will have to attend the other's funeral. And once again suffer through the crushing loss of someone we care deeply for. I'm not sure that I've made it clear how often this subject comes up between me and my widowed friends. Some say they just can't take that chance again nor handle going through that loss again. For us widowers to start over we must first come to terms with this issue. Maybe we don't ever completely solve it but we at least try to be at peace with the fact it could happen. I am now convinced that this is the main reason we are afraid to commit to another relationship.

The second part of this matter is by taking that step we worry we are perceived as giving up on the memory of our lost spouse. That is simply not posssible. Our lives are fully woven together. Their memory never goes away just because we choose to live our way to the end instead of spending the rest of our lives alone. To forget them would mean we would have to forget 40 years of our own lives. Just not possible.

Let me make this point even more clear. We still miss our spouses. Every day. Sometimes when we are with you and even occasionally when we are with each other. The longing to see them one more time never ends. But we do have to gently tuck our loved ones away in a safe place. In a corner of our memory that only we can access. So we can live in the moment and not the past. (Because I have now come to realize that you cannot live in the present while completely focused on someone who no longer exists.) Then in those times when we truly need them, we can always pull that memory back to the surface.

Actually there is another side to this second part. It was relayed to me by my father last spring. Somehow we had managed to begin a discussion about me seeing someone again. I had previously told him I didn't feel I would ever find someone who would measure up to Mom. I also added that I just wouldn't feel right about seeing them even if I did. (I should point out that he and Grandma loved your mother like she was their own.) His reply was certainly not what I was expecting. He looked me in the eye and said, "I hope you haven't completely given up on the idea of finding someone special. And maybe it's time I explain some things to you."(Coming from your father that's about as threatening as when a woman says, "we need to talk".) He continued. "I get the feeling from our discussions that you're not even looking for another companion because you believe that when you get to Heaven, your relationships will be the same as they were here on earth. And you aren't really looking because you feel that would somehow be breaking your marriage vows and your promises to Cheryl. I believe the Bible is very clear on this point. When you get to Heaven it is likely that you and she will recognize and love each other but you will never be married again. That only happens here. In Heaven you will be married to Jesus and His church and living on a higher level of existence than we are capable of living here. And do I need to remind you of the line, "till death do us part?" We know you loved her. That was so obvious. But she's not coming back. If you think you would be betraying Cheryl, you need to get past that. And if you don't believe me then get out your Bible and read Matthew 22 verses 23-30."

I believe this mini-sermon from my father was yet another attempt by God to get my attention and to straighten out my misinterpretation of His Word. The timing was so very important! Although I hadn't really put much significance into our conversation until a few short days later when I received a request to meet for a simple visit. And I then had the opportunity to ask a certain lady out to dinner. I realized how much I missed being part of a couple. And just how lonely I had become. Though my heart would likely never fully recover from losing someone a second time. I am willing to take that risk. I'm betting it's worth every moment we have together. No matter how long that is.

We both worry that God knew just how quickly we would move to join our lives. We've discussed that maybe He intended for us to do just that. Because maybe He knows one or both of us don't have much time left here. That feeling of dread and fear is also something we have discussed. We often sense that this new relationship is so good that we wonder if it can last. We came from such a low place in our lives to a high that some never reach. Especially twice in a lifetime. Some will get to this place quicker than us and some will never get here. We all travel at a different speed in our journey. Ours is a journey once tested by loss , now tested by gain. We are hoping we'll be able to somehow carry on if loss is again in our near future. I know that either way, I'll have been a better version of me for having the experience of getting to know her.

No regrets. Not one.

CHAPTER FOURTEEN

:

I WANNA WIN!

I eat lunch almost every day with a bunch of "steer jockeys". And because 99% of the population doesn't know what that means, I'm gonna explain that term. At our local coffee shop, just like many across this land, there is a large table in the center of the room with smaller tables surrounding it. When you enter you have to choose if you are going to sit with random customers in the middle or if you want a little privacy and want to sit at one of the outlying spots. Those small tables are not really that private but the folks at the center table have to at least work a little harder to hear your conversation. Which they will certainly do if key words or phrases are overheard. These include but aren't limited to: farm for sale, farm for rent, divorce etc.

I generally sit at the center table where you are subjected to whatever discussions and criticisms are taking place. (It also seems to be where the waitresses and customers believe any comments made are fair game for exaggerations and enhancements, as needed.) Besides the steer jocks there are also usually several of the local "characters" in attendence. This sometimes includes the wondering soul who refers to himself as "Old Wise One".(I've never actually heard anyone call him that except himself but we tolerate the description anyway.) He is a retired, vest wearing tree logger who travels the country in old Ford pickups until his wife misses him too much(so he says) or until his current allotment of clean clothes fails him. He then returns and offers up observations and wisdom to us less worldly travelers. (He also claims to have graduated from Harvard at the top of his class at age 16 and to hold several international pole vault records.) He then picks up another of his trucks (he has four), a garbage bag full of clean clothes and takes off again. Mostly he travels west until he hits an ocean or at least a mountain, turns left(south), circles California or Arizona and returns back through Texas and Missouri. He never goes east from home. And he almost always turns left. Some wonder if he wasn't a buffalo in a past life or even a Nascar driver?

Now back to the steer jocks. They are cattle loving farmers, their children, hired helpers and student interns from a local junior college. And they love to show, display, sell, buy and compete with their cows, bulls, heifers and especially steers. At the local, county, state and national cattle shows. They haggle about judges, breeds, show rings and hair. But mostly they argue about the winners and losers at the latest shows. They are unbelievably competitive and showing cattle is often what they want to discuss at the center table.

For those of you who have never attended a livestock show, it's kind of like a beauty pageant where cattle,(and sometimes hogs, sheep, chickens, goats and rabbits) are paraded around all "dolled up", while a judge observes them and eventually places them in order of top to bottom place. They "fluffem" and "puffem" and even blow dry them in something called a "cooler".(It's sort of like a cold hair salon for cattle that makes their hair grow faster.) Trust me, these show cattle are treated like kings and queens. Because it's not about the meat or the muscle or even the steaks folks. From what I can tell, it's all about the hair!

And what does showing cattle have to do with my story? Lately, I can relate to those show critters and their being on display. Because lately I've felt like I've been on the show circuit myself. Since I started seeing my lady friend I've been introduced to her children, the grandchildren, neices, nephews, cousins, aunts and uncles, friends, former colleagues, her pastor, the assistant pastor, the landscaper, the guy who mows her lawn, and the gal who rubs her feet! (Has something to do with making her teeth feel better but when I asked her if brushing her teeth made her toes tickle she gave me one of those "looks." You know, the one that says , "that's a really stupid question".) I think I've been exhibited and introduced to about everyone but the pool boy. And I better never meet him cause she doesn't even have a pool!

No one has had the nerve to tell me yet just what position I've achieved in this show. But I am sure of one thing. If I am being judged on the basis of my overall body structure or the soundness of my feet, I'm in trouble here. I wouldn't even win best hair. For sure, not Grand Champion. Probably not even Reserve Champion. Heck, I'd just be happy to win my weight class. You know, the "Old, gray haired, worn out, over 200 pounds, with a bit of foot rot class". I want to at least be able to tell the grandchildren I won that one!

And hopefully before their parents put me out to pasture.

CHAPTER FIFTEEN

:

MAYBE IT'S TIME

You say you can see it in our faces and our eyes. You say we seem more settled. You can tell by the way we carry ourselves. We seem to laugh more easily and often. You say that it's obvious to everyone what was missing has now been found. We had no idea. No idea that what we are feeling on the inside can be seen on the outside too. We only know that we are happier than we've been since losing our spouses. We walk a fine line. A line between wanting to show you how happy we are in our new lives and wanting to be respectful of those who came before us.

Along with our newly found joy comes new questions and uncertainty. Not just for us but for you, our children. We are keenly aware of that. And we know you are striving to be excited with us while struggling to not feel guilty for what you view as betrayal of your lost parents. We know you have to work through those thoughts as we have had to work through them also.

Will he/she try to be my mom/dad ? He/She is always around so how can we talk like we used to? Can I just stop by or do I have to call first? What about the holidays? Where will you be then? Will his/her kids become more important than me? Does he/she treat you well? Do you really love him/her? Is this serious? And most importantly, have you forgotten about Mom/Dad? I'm sure these and many more questions have crossed your minds since we started this new relationship. Legitimate questions that we don't always have answers to. With important choices to make. (I assumed that children of divorced parents have many of the same questions and choices. When I expressed that to a young man who'd experienced divorce, he reminded me that he was just a child when his parents divorced and really didn't have the option to disagree. Now many years later and his mother seeing someone new, he did have that choice. And having choices actually may make adjusting to the current situation even harder.)

At this time I would like to directly address some of those questions. And while I still don't have all the answers, I feel it's time to try to assure you of what I do know about our new relationship.

To my Children

I loved your mother and will always love her and you, our children. I will never forget her and the countless memories we share. But, I believe I have room in my heart and my life for another special person. And as I told you a long time ago, I "chose"your mother. Not you. So you need to trust my instincts. We did pretty well the last time.

To her Children

I will always treat your mother with respect. Even when I may disagree with her. My parents and my wife taught me just how important that is. If I can't do that then I believe I am in the wrong place with the wrong person and should move on.

To Our Children

We do not want to replace your mother or father. We believe that you only get one of each in a lifetime and know that we are not that person for you. Our only hope is that we can become your friend and we know that we must earn that.

We now realize we had become terribly lonely since losing your mom/dad and because of that have grown to appreciate the little things we once took for granted. But we are human and expect that you will remind us when we do fall back into old habits of not appreciating each other.

We intend to be open and honest about our feelings and hope that you will do the same. The lack of communication will certainly be our downfall.

We hope you will give us the chance to know each other. Even though we did not begin our lives together, we believe we all want the same ending. To get back to a "near normal" life and to be happy again.

Finally, we hope we never get overly confident and take our place in your lives for granted. We know where we stand. We know we are living in the shadows, cast by the pedestal you've placed our predecessors on. Yet we are often and sadly reminded they won't return. And we believe we can love someone new for totally different reasons than we loved your parents. For we are in totally different places in our lives.

We know how much their memory means to you. Because it also means so much to us. And we believe we are in this position because God has placed us here for a purpose we don't yet know or understand. Hopefully you can tell how happy we are. Not only by our appearance but by the actions we take. So maybe it's time. Time to make some decisions about the rest of our lives. Looking far into the future for a change. Just maybe it's time to decide if we'll die of a broken heart, or go forward with a cracked one?

CHAPTER SIXTEEN

:

THE FINAL CHAPTER?

Prayer. Simply having a conversation with God. Ultimately that and faith are what have carried me through the last six years. Though I've known Him for more than 40 years it never ceases to amaze me that in this world of 7+ billion people, He even has time to listen to my call. It is as if I am the last person left on this earth as He singles me out and hears my every thought. Only He has that ability. He's always there and waiting for me to reach out. Always seemingly eager to hear of my joys and my concerns. I've had many of both since losing Mom. And I've experienced tremendous changes in my life. None more frightening and yet fulfilling than the relationship I recently began.

Certainly life isn't fair. As I've often heard my pastor say, "If it was, then we'd die in the order in which we are born." It just doesn't work that way. Losing Mom has changed me forever. In some ways it has knocked me down and I've had to muster the courage to stand back up. In some ways it has been the catalyst for lifting me up and giving me the strength to carry on.

I believe everyone and everything has a purpose. And I believe God has one in mind for me. That story is already written though I am not sure what it is. I do now know that these letters have become my voice. My way of expressing what I don't feel well prepared to do verbally. To tell people what losing your spouse is truly like. And the changes you must endure. And maybe most important, the joys that are still possible.

There are several reasons for God to put me where I am today. In this situation. In this exact place in time. Maybe one of them is to set the example that there still can be hope. Even at my age. Even when you live in a cornfield. I finally do believe my life did not end when I lost Mom. And I feel I can look ahead with the determination of living life to it's fullest again. It's time for another new chapter to begin. Moving forward with Mom's memory always with me. Not moving on without her. But carrying her forever with me as I go.

My girlfriend and I feel we have lost so much. If you genuinely loved your spouse that's what happens with their loss. Although we don't know exactly where we are headed and with no guarantees this will work, we have decided to try and live each day along the journey as if it could be our last. Traveling the path together. Savoring each moment we have. For we know, better than some that time is a gift. And some day this too will end.

For those friends who in the beginning of this new relationship felt I should hold something back, I have these questions. Which part do you believe I should have held in reserve? The part where we talked into the early morning hours? The part where I expressed my fears of losing someone again? Or maybe the part where we've held each other while enduring yet another yearly milestone of loss? I can't do that. You know I'm not built that way. When I commit to something I hold nothing back. Regardless of the outcome.

And while some who haven't experienced our loss may think we've moved too fast, we are afraid we may have moved too slowly and taken too long to find each other. We fear our lack of time may catch us all too soon. (I even wrote this last chapter before I finished the rest because of my fear that something might happen to keep me from it.)

I pray to God every day to give me strength and faith. Strength to look back and remember how much my first relationship meant to me. And faith to look forward to what could be again.

See ya later,

Dad